ASSARACUS

A Journal of Gay Poetry
Issue 05

Alexander, Arkansas
WWW.SIBLINGRIVALRYPRESS.COM

Assaracus
A Journal of Gay Poetry
Issue 5: January 2012
ISBN: 978-1-937420-10-9
ISSN: 2159-0478
Bryan Borland, Editor
Brent Calderwood, Associate Editor
Philip F. Clark, Art Editor
Copyright © 2012 by Sibling Rivalry Press

Cover Art: "Wounded Soldier" by Paul Pinkman. Used by Permission.

All rights reserved. No part of this journal may be reproduced or republished without written consent from the publisher, except by reviewers who may quote brief excerpts in connection with a review in a newspaper, magazine, or electronic publication; nor may any part of this journal be reproduced, stored in a retrieval system, or transmitted in any form without written consent of the publisher. However, contributors maintain ownership rights of their individual poems and as such retain all rights to publish and republish their work.

Sibling Rivalry Press, LLC
13913 Magnolia Glen Drive
Alexander, AR 72002

www.siblingrivalrypress.com

Assaracus Issue 05

The Poems of Perry Brass
p. 6

The Poems of Guillermo Filice Castro
p. 16

The Poems of Vicente Molina Foix
Translated from the Spanish by Lawrence Schimel
p. 25

The Poems of Christopher Gaskins
p. 36

The Poems of Michael Hathaway
p. 49

The Poems of Matthew R. Loney
p. 61

The Poems of Jeff Mann
p. 77

The Poems of Jory M. Mickelson
p. 94

The Poems of Erik Schuckers
p. 105

The Poems of Kat Smalley
p. 119

The Poems of David-Glen Smith
p. 128

Featuring the Art of Paul Pinkman
Artist's Biography p. 143

PERRY BRASS

PERFECT FUTURE

PERRY BRASS is a poet, novelist, playwright, and activist originally from Savannah, Georgia. He has published 15 books, winning numerous awards for his poetry, plays, and fiction. He has been involved in the movement for LGBT rights since November of 1969, when he co-edited *Come Out!*, the world's first gay liberation newspaper, published by the Gay Liberation Front of New York. In 1972, with two friends he started the Gay Men's Health Project Clinic, the first clinic for gay men on the East Coast, still operating as New York's Callen-Lorde. The clinic, operating from a basement in New York's West Village, strongly advocated the use of condoms by gay men a decade before the advent of AIDS, even though most gay men still considered them to be only a birth control device. Brass's work often deals with an intersection of sexuality, spirituality and personal politics that came directly, openly, out of his involvement with the radical queer politics of the late 1960s and early 1970s. This intersection was deemed "impossible" by many academics and even gay activists of the early years of the movement, who could accept one but none of the other elements that now make up the LGBT movement. He is currently a coordinator of the Rainbow Book Fair, the only LGBT book fair in the U.S. His essay, "A Distant Memory: Andrew Bifrost and *Mouth of the Dragon*," which appeared in *Ganymede Unfinished*, was the inspiration behind *Assaracus*.

www.perrybrass.com

CNIDARIAN*

All speckled with light
and jelly and silvered flecks of salt,
all twisting and gliding
and catching drools
of amber before they fall
into grist along the sand: it shoots
a spew of water and wriggles forward,
menacing, floating close. Who says
beauty is simple? Complicate me,
detain me. Make me afraid; I will gasp
to catch my breath, then bloat
with air to come up, to become one
with your layer beneath the waves,
where sunlight is refracted
in my observant pulse, where any dream
is lethal until the night
sucks the tide through its course.

December 14, 2003
Bronx, NY

---

*Cnidarian (C is silent) - pertaining to the invertebrate phylum *Cnidaria*: jellyfish, hydras, sea anemones, and corals.

INTOXICANTS

There I am: giddy in the hormonal pool
    of being young, listening to people
flushed with the liquors of their passions,
egos glistening, stroked, on fire: All new!
All ready! And the money of it, rushing, waiting,
easy if only I'd reach for it, and who wouldn't?
Shouldn't? So we join the stream—the years
                      back then,

the disco beats, the songs, the beaches
and bathing suits, the alcohol and suntan lotion,
nights of listening in cars and lights
beaming around you, you beaming,
loving it for being loved for being you . . .
                  you! . . .
fresh, silly, too serious but standing
up now: it was easy, this glamour
of every generation from Van Dyck
to the latest thing that emerges

as a spot on the horizon, slick
with promise, speeding in its
                perfect future
aimed to claim an audience,
to be swallowed, heated by your own
            appetite, and so
eager to elude you.

December 14, 2009
5:34 A.M.
Bronx, NY

MILK
for Gus Van Sant and Jeffrey Lann Campbell*

Like the pink, enameled reaches of a conch shell
to my ear, this has caused me to hear
my people, those I have loved
with the blood of my soul; but this is something cold,
hard, physical, real—to pull the past out
of my guts and bring back its color from
the dust of books, newsprint, and old stories,
now alive like dreams and the fevered colors
of those nineteenth century agit-prop paintings
by Delacroix, Gericault, Girodet, making heroic
what was comic, making even more mythic
what was merely echo. And I

have begun to confuse the crowded screen
with my own memory that is visceral,
swelling to unleash itself from the pain
of longing and regret into the splendor
of full recall: the very people who once
walked with me and I can feel their hands
on my face and neck, pressing
my skin, my fingers, with their smiles
and great intentions, their dreams compacted
by stifling limits and then released
into the surging pressure of a million energies:
that density of physical desire
                becoming real by revelation
                        and exposure
to the rush of courage, of what can
and must be, what can be taken
and brought to the feet of the governed
                who will see themselves
                      now starkly
as pure, individual, worthy: this awakened power

---

*Gus Van Sant directed the 2008 film *Milk* about gay activist Harvey Milk. Jeffrey Lann Campbell was a gay activist from Charlotte, North Carolina, who became the director of the New Orleans Stop AIDS Task Force in the early 90s. Jeffrey died of AIDS in 1993. He was the poet's best friend.

splurged without embarrassment
into the eyes of the almost dead,
sleeping, too comfortably napping,
through the freezing storm of evasion.
Wake up! It had to happen! Put some steel
into your backs and eyelids. Don't be afraid,
      even through the insistence of fear
that stings you like salt—you can channel
through it, and dip your tongue
into truth and taste its own sweet,
      home-washed flesh.
You were meant to be this thing—I
saw it—knew it—in the hollow of my youth
as youth knows it again and again,
dreaming of waking up to it,
and then waking boldly, and I listened
to you and to others, and I can
feel you on my forehead
and your fingers in my hand,
and hold the slight, quick blush
of your breath on my ankles in
the dark, or the rain on my naked shoulders
in the summer in New York
when I took my shirt off
in the drench of memories
having left Savannah, Georgia,
for the big city to become a man.

December 31, 2008
2:54 A.M.
Bronx, NY

A LIFE WITHOUT MONEY

You're alive—and every pore of you
is open to a thousand possibilities, fantastic
calibrations of a world that won't end with you,
but will go on in its illusions while you watch
       amazed, beguiled as a four year old
learning to attach signs to meanings, but of you—
what can you attach, to make your dumb yearnings succeed
in the wreck of reality—you, now in this elixir of euphoria
arising in its own adrenalized fury to the very
edge of hysteria—how could you help it, and why?
       Picasso ate ruthlessly and painted
with his teeth, pecker, and scrotum—
       so it occurred to you. *You?*
                        You—
who were you in this maelstrom,
in this sack of your own, engorged self?
The artist within you rebelled and the wizard smirked.
Neither had answers, while the vulgar monster
that you hid in your ambitions, clothed in clichés
and accepted by half-wits, the thing that educated you
from its own plight and window-show of experience,
              told you: accept no consequences
other than how *you* can bend circumstances.

Accept this as a prayer, a thing clerical and magical,
a work of art that you can climb into and constitute
with your own clandestine acts, refingered now
like a Bach cantata on the grounds of renewable religion.

How do you do it—and live? Murder would be complicated
and messy, and the energy you'd need to take anything
            would never exceed the gain.
You did a little study, a flow chart, an imbecilic
squandering, practical as a traffic ticket,
and all that you arrived at was—staying alive
menaces you, despite your own glistening delight
       which presently defines you: too
pretty to excuse away, it's too lovely to let wither,
and you're sad that it might deflate like a soufflé
when your own heat has been siphoned
by the jokes and dicks of working stiffs: Ahh!

Perry Brass

The confounded truth: wars are exactly waged
                              for this,
to keep jerks like you engaged and stoking
in a scheme that makes no sense, has no outcome,
but keeps you fed, clothed, and silly with
        its own stupifications. O', adventure!
        And the swindle that calls itself
by so many names: political morality;
a "life plan" nailed to your bank account;
and "tunnel vision," remember that?
They threw you in a pit and packed the hole with dirt—
you were reminded you needed it: only look at the good,
    the big win, a perfect society washed clean
of unreliables—that scam, you worked with *that*,
                              ate it, lived on it

            while life,
more enchanting than any gilt-edged bubble
eluded you. It was not in your tunnel, what they
dug for you. You were deceived, mutilated, and let go
        with a flow of Christian sympathy:
all crap and phony—sure, you knew it, but stayed
too deep in your blowhole to show it.

Or know it.

Till you burrowed out, all bile and craziness—
with nothing left to lose except some last
illusion of controlled perfection. And that stank
as you sank into penury.   But a distant light
straight from the asshole of darkness faced you—
It blinked neon pink and white: Starvation
                like a tape worm
                would
                EAT
                you,
unless you learned to lie with the best of them,
reclining among the liars, while groping to snip
    their own grapes: the twits at work
who on occasion only claimed their silvery traces
in the john, flushing down daily with the shit
their own starry selves, the self they dodged
late at night, winking back at them
from bitter dreams. Flush! Gone!

Perry Brass

                You thought
about running drugs or marrying for money—
who doesn't?   But both by definition

devour the truth of you, leaving only for evidence
some silky membrane left from your own smile. So

you chose to be a mercenary in a mercenary time
and got away with it, until the eyes of the kids who died

          soaked you in such anguish
that your stomach turned raw from heaving
and your nuts shriveled from revulsion. You
were an outcast again. You'd blown your own in-
dependence, bought at the price of servitude.

But—so many men who go in for ideals only end up
        in cruelty: you knew it. You were smart
enough to see it, in that same path of virtue that
had brought you on this course: the one where you
could touch yourself and claim your own bright soul.
                      Shithead!
You'd put to sword your own hunger then fed it
with monstrosity, still any decent developer
has a better story. Count on it. So you were left

with piddling alternatives: drop out in a commune,
make tofu ice cream for tourists in Kansas,
become a Jesus-dope or a monk bruised by his own
perversions of sensuality: pain, deprivation, prayer.

                    You
                    knew
                    it,
               you could
                    DO
                    it,
if you had to—to preserve that little piece of you
you'd allow no one else to buy— lucky you!
You believed in "authenticity" before it
got offered on the Shopping Network or
the girly yoga catalogs sent out weekly
from marketers in Reno. You had it: you could see it,
this little face of yours with the bird wings
attached and the eyes blue as oranges, blue

as honey from the deepest ocean, and you
                              didn't want it
                              to leave you
no matter what the cost or penalty. You
would have to lie to the liars and outpriest
all the priests, you would have to be ruthless
to uncarapace yourself *if* only to you. How
              lonely it was, small as that delicious
narcissism of responsibility choking you, stuffing
itself with your own marrow and shitting out
                        your daily sorrow.

Finally, you decided—trippy, giddy, renewed
by your own charm—to join the happy throngs,
witless as they were but enjoying their own
business, gleeful as the Bronx fans after a shut-out
Yankees game—wherever there is religion
                    in the daily seeking of oblivion,
you went for it. You tilted yourself upside down
to do it, burrowing deep into your own weakness.
                        It was so safe.
Sleep without death. Just do it! A degree
of Nazarene charity like a cigarette before
a firing squad or a loan against a gambling debt—
so: you will not drown. You went on like this,
a blind traveler speaking only to the blind.

You decided to renounce money, become ascetic,
live on the beach. Like a bleached surfer dude.
You parked cars, cleaned houses, stole lawn stuff
from the rich and tithed to the poor, to homeless
men who knew a lot but sadly nothing at all. You
studied God and saw nothing good in it,
except the same blind alleys. But one day

                    on the beach
I got enlightened as a storm came in,
swelling the air until it broke upon me
like a temper, pouring rain as a beneficence
                    upon my skin.
I smiled. Life is short. We are blessed with it
but most are too poor to know it. They run after
everything including the fatalities of destiny.
They are bereft of love and bankrupt of all
human richness. They spend zillions on the blind

pursuits of art instead of the living pursuits
of experience—of seeing and being.
Love was as merciless as hate, but more pleasant
to curl within its clutches. This I learned. This
was a life without money.

July 23, 2010
Bronx, NY

GUILLERMO FILICE CASTRO

A Blunt Unevenness of Flesh

GUILLERMO FILICE CASTRO is the author of two chapbooks, *Cry Me a Lorca* (Seven Kitchens Press, Summer Series 2010) and *Toy Storm* (Big Fat Press, 1997). Of the poems represented here, "Mom Poem (vii)" was previously published in the Fall 2010 issue of *The Bellevue Literary Review*. Other work has appeared in *Barrow Street*, *Bloom*, *The Brooklyn Rail*, *Court Green*, *Quarterly West*, and elsewhere, as well as in the anthologies *My Diva*, *This Full Green Hour*, *Saints of Hysteria*, and more. His translations of Argentine poet Olga Orozco, in collaboration with Ron Drummond, have been featured in *Guernica*, *Terra Incognita*, *U.S. Latino Review*, and *Visions*. A native of Argentina, he is now a full-fledged American citizen.

TO THE DEPORTADOS

Those of us
Who dodged the raids
Pick up your shift your broom
Continue mixing water with blood
Under carcasses of today's beef
We do not like it but
Deal in Jersey in Miami in LA
Anywhere the might of our Lady
Of the Green might
Take us
We who followed the human snout
Of sleek coyotes
Have learned to
Be mobile and fleet
And burn the crosshairs off
Each other's backs
When the necessary papers are forged
With typos and whatnot
We are reborn
In a Corona
Queens
Butcher's back room
Other identifying details withheld
We must as we bust
Moves
In a number of accents
Pass fliers
And snarl at the stars
Thumbing through a night
Taut and cold as the flag on the moon
Hermanitos Hermanitas
Be patient or just plainly be
Enjoy the temporary ousting
And may you all safely sneak back in

MOM POEM (i)

"Sense of purpose" is the last thing I believe;
actually quite

good at *Who Am I Kidding?*-myself (and)
dropping anvils in the pond
the water always restores
itself regardless the tool descends (in disbelief)

[she introduced me to water, I to swimming]

The images are
her Voice   (disbelief)
clear-
ly I'm not dreaming (did I say) disbelief
because of the distance

I tell myself I've developed a "new set of skills"
(disbelief) to cope with her
[now]   [she
introduced me to disbelief, I to distance]

-Now-   (/Constriction=DifficultBreathing/)
Now/in/death: Now/her/death: Now:

(This dis-)   distant

belief
I'm not (dreaming)
so small but [for now] pour me for eternity
into her dish-washing gloves

MOM POEM (ii)

It is in your house again
Hanging over
The unfamiliar edge of your duvet
The same quiet you loved
Following clean rooms
Where you reigned like a child
Skilled at buffing tiles and sprinkling
Poison on roses laden with ants
That faded under
The only pink snow they would ever know

MOM POEM (iii)

As the wave caught you unawares
And lifted you from behind
This buoyant partner
Then split and slid around
Your hips
To dress you
In flamenco ruffles
      And whatever utterance
Your mouth pitched
Toward a triad of clouds
Made your whole chest
Push and surge forward
Joyfully
My Latin Ursula Andress
In front of the camera
Nothing but loose-lipped shells
Beneath your imperfect arches

MOM POEM (iv)

The lady they pulled from the water
She lay in her green bikini as if boneless on the grass
Liquid bubbled under the cork placed between
Her purple lips its purpose unknown
A doctor perhaps hesitated over her like a wasp
What to do but watch as no one was allowed back in the pool
I see why this pops in my head today
Forty-odd years
And six thousand miles of Atlantic Ocean later
While on the phone long distance with you
Carping about the endless heat wave
In a rapid slippery shallow speech
On the last hours of your life
Well water has always bound us
Since we once broke it together
When I towed you across a pool
Hoping as I hopped backwards you'd learn to float
The way you now move into a lightness
Beyond clumsy strokes

MOM POEM (v)

> "Nobody wants to die, and at the same time nobody wants to die badly."
> From the PBS program Frontline: Facing Death.

The thing with her body
She didn't want family to see:
The one breast
That got really small.

She didn't want family to see
Under her oversized shirt
What got really small
One cup size at a time.

Under her oversized shirt
She nursed a secret
That capsized at the time
She tried on a tighter blouse.

She nursed secrets
Don't we all?
And had on a tighter blouse.
Someone snapped her picture.

And don't we all
Choose when and what to see?
Someone snapped the picture
Family failed to notice.

Choose where and what to see:
The rest gets cropped out of the shot.
Family failed to notice
The blunt unevenness of flesh.

The rest got cropped out of the shot.
The left breast,
A blunt unevenness of flesh;
That thing in her body. That thing.

MOM POEM (vi)

A single engine
From the nearby flight school
Whirs up in the blue
And cues in
The only time she'll move under the rented shade
Together we
Push cold meat through crust
And cloud-like dough
She points out
The German lifeguard's impeccable
Heel-to-toe
Stride toward the showers
Against my own flat-footed
Blunders
On track and field
The plane jerks left
Akin to a husband sharply elbowed
For excessive snoring
Despite many warnings
I bleed
Blood oranges get sticky
Tip knuckle and shin
She fuels the baby in me
With understated giddiness
So regal and alien
Are we
To the rhino beetles on the grass
Pitching horns into our rubber slippers
And the spoils of lunch

MOM POEM (vii)

You were in love with doctors,
You crazy gal in need of doctors,
You obsessed with fictional doctors

Whose constant doctor-on-doctor
Action lured in more potent doctors.
And how they tickled you, doctors.

Or nurses, falling for the wrong doctors!
You could never have enough doctors,
All made up but lab-coated as actual doctors,

Who nonetheless could doctor
Your see-saw mind to Doctor-is-
Blessed and Doctor-is-

Best perfection... soon that doctor
Routine soured you on prop doctors
Until a new, valor-and-Valium giving real doctor

Could flip you like no other doctor.
From then on your litany of *El Doctor
Said This, El Doctor Said That* dialed the doctor

Number to the next level of doctor
Madness in our household: Doctors
Made to order, invisible witch doctors

Justly good to you, fragile, unequivocal, all those doctors.

VICENTE MOLINA FOIX

TRANSLATED FROM THE SPANISH
BY LAWRENCE SCHIMEL

PROHIBITION RULES

VINCENTE MOLINA FOIX is a Spanish author, critic, and film director. He belongs to the generation of "Novísimo" poets and was included in the canonic anthology *Nueve novísimos poetas españoles* edited by José María Castellnet in 1970. He is primarily a novelist; his most recent, *El abrecartas* (The Letter Opener), won the National Literature Prize. His numerous honors include the Premio Herralde, Premio Azorín, Premio Barral, among others. He has translated many works into Spanish, including important versions of Shakespeare (*Hamlet*, *King Lear*, *The Merchant of Venice*). His first two films as writer and director are *Sagitario* (Sagitarius) and *El dios de madera* (The Wooden God).

LAWRENCE SCHIMEL was born in New York City and is currently living in Madrid, Spain. He is an award-winning author and anthologist who has published over 100 books in a wide variety of genres, including fiction, cooking, gender studies, sports, poetry, and comics. He is the publisher of A Midsummer Night's Press.

A LIMBO

I say goodbye to you
until next
month,
at least.
A breather.
Let's give ourselves a breather.
Of course I already know
that we will
sleep together
again soon.
But for now I enjoy,
you enjoy,
may we both enjoy
the limbo.

And not because
to live with you
is an inferno,
it's not.
Rather it's that
from the place
where the innocents purge themselves
of the guilt of not having
passed in time
the baptism
of fire
of love,
I want to dream a little
more
of that heaven
which lovers
say
that we have
(almost all of us)
promised to us.

Vicente Molina Foix – translated by Lawrence Schimel

BIRTHDAY WITHOUT YOU

I see you and my heart
no longer jumps
like it used to jump
in hope of a glance from you.

I see you and now I don't run
to write new verses
reconstructing the kiss
you didn't manage to give me.

I see you and now I can
talk without saying anything,
impossible before,
for my voice gave me away.

I look at you and before my eyes
there no longer crosses
that procession of the dream
of embracing you closely.

I embrace you and there no longer beats
beneath your flesh
that invisible soul
I could one day hear.

I touch you and no longer feel.
I look at you and no longer see.
I hear you and no longer pay heed.
You leave and I don't turn sour.

Vicente Molina Foix – translated by Lawrence Schimel

BLIND ANTINOUS

Illuminated statue.
Thus, your white eyes
see the rug
woven in the museum's paving stones
by the lover.

Your restored body
is not of marble
alone.
Clay from my steps has clung
to the clay of the artist's hand.

He made you, and found,
although two centuries had already passed,
the pained disdain of your gesture
and the near absence of who
demanded your face be printed
on the coins.

I observe the three of you,
and then
the artist's hand splashes me,
your curly hair sets mine to stand on end,
the unquiet lover speaks to my lover's restlessness.

But the shoes
of the guard,
and his master key,
come to shut you down.
It's time.
And without the artifice of the electric lights
you are nothing.
The artist's art ends at the pedestal.
He who was so faithful to you no longer looks at the stars
to see if you still love him.
I leave the room
behind the tourists
who have stumbled upon your image
in search of a saner god.

THE CALL OF THE FLESH

Two knocks at the door.
I ignore it.
I know you,
downstairs neighbor,
base passion,
and today I am not going to answer.
Try tomorrow and see
if you have luck.

You usually appear
without warning,
and that is a lack of
consideration.
I treat you well,
I try to pleasure you,
show you off
with the best bodies
of the moment.
I have even paid
so that you were not
so alone.
And you assail yet again.
You don't even use
a password.
I hear your lame steps
on the stairway,
and later the tock-tock.
You come with haste, Desire,
and you don't care at all
for anything I am in the midst of.
You call like a soldier
who has won a war
and returns home
to occupy the room
that a meek mother
kept clean.

I no longer wait for you.
I am seriously trying
to quit myself
of that vice
of being

yours.
And I even want to close
the bedroom
where for many years
I kept you
as a half-boarder.
I've grown older.
I no longer need you.
Let me be, you hanger-on.
Don't you see you're distracting me
from my tasks?
Go with those who still
take you up
for your novelty.
To me you are already
over-familiar.
Don't you have
another face
to offer me?
Once and for all, go down
to the basement of walls
stained
with humidity
where your insane empire
is safe.
Here, in the castle
of my body,
from this night on,
Prohibition
rules.

MATCHMAKING

Over the years
I have become
a superb
matchmaker
of ex
beaus.

In the most-populous cities
of three countries,
I visit
stable couples
who hold hands
gratefully
and have the grace to keep me
on the altars
of their dressers
with a photo
from back then,
a flattering shot.
I have come to count
in happy homes,
six books dedicated
by me
with promises
of eternal love.

And in one recent case
I could recognize
the hand-knitted coat
I gave my lover
for Christmas
worn by his new man,
and some of my vomit stains
on the parquet
of that bedroom
which is forbidden to me these days.
I am the visitor
of the love-struck.

If it is true, as you say,
you, conscience,
who can't lie,

Vicente Molina Foix – translated by Lawrence Schimel

that I no longer know how to love,
at least admit
that I prepare those I reject
quite well
for the tricky tests
of true love.

Vicente Molina Foix – translated by Lawrence Schimel

REENCOUNTERING THE BELOVED IN A SECONDHAND BOOKSHOP

So then,
once
our time together
was through,
you continued reading.

And I had thought
that it was only because of me,
thanks to my influence and well
stocked
library,
that you had begun to open
books.

Could I have made
you into
a luminary?
A future
genius
of letters?

I can't manage to read
the spines of
the tomes
you're glancing at.
But I vow:
the next time
I am not going to give away
just like that
the only thing I keep
up with,
bibliography.

SECOND EPIGRAM

They tell me that you sleep
with everyone.
And those who I meet
tell me
that
they have had you
in their arms.
To all of them you speak of me
as you undress.

But when these heroes
of a single conquest
depict you,
I refuse
to recognize you.
I don't remember
those lips
which according to them are red
and which I found prone
to sores
and too white
for your country.
Nor did your hair
ever seem to me
chestnut brown,
but rather almost black
and with dandruff.

Vicente Molina Foix – translated by Lawrence Schimel

SYNESTHESIA

In the sonorous
color of
the lips
that I can't even kiss,
nor care to open
for me
their gates,
I try the anesthesia
of a strong
drug, as strong as
ignored
love.

The halt rhyme
of the verses
which that soul *other* sings,
to whose sound
I sleep
to not awaken
or to wake
like a blind
stone state
carved
with a single hand
by a child.

CHRISTOPHER GASKINS

A Spotlight in Daydreams

CHRISTOPHER GASKINS was born and raised in southwest Florida, then moved to New York City in 1999, looking for the hustle and bustle he'd always heard so much about. He currently lives in Brooklyn, where he teaches high school English, as well as a writing course at a local college. His poems have appeared in such journals as *The Gay & Lesbian Review Worldwide*, *Ganymede*, *Open Minds Quarterly*, *Darkling*, *Pearl*, *Chroma*, and in the anthologies *Sanctified* and *Gay City, vol. 2*.

DANCING ALONE WITH DARREN

There is no
body, only flesh
for miles
unseen by eyes and

gripped,
a grudge with a dagger's
plunge, an
eightball eye roll

and flaccid feint.
Beguiled
in turn with the bile to bear
bizarre ingrown

burns, each pelting-rain
kiss
like this to hit your
asphalt angles,

smooth, smoldering shoulders,
groped
for lust and a surge
like hair.

Daring discordance or a
liquid-eyed look,
confusion in
pupils now widening, livid

around the quick, pin-
prick of effort,
wetter
than depth, waiting longer to linger,

fall
closer to this: the snap
of air
between us broken.

THE SPIDER-WOMAN

It wasn't death
that took you away from yearning fans
who wrote in letters of
admiration, adoration, words of hope
which flowed and
had nowhere else to go.
I never wrote

although late at night and past my bedtime,
curled up small
in fetal form underneath
the blankets, you would rise again in crimson, black,
and yellow
to soar in shadows and ride the breezes
on gossamer wings,

to stand against the world's mosaic
of super-villains
and ward away with your grim expressions the
loneliness
and a need for love which always were
the worst of all.
I would smile, then turn the page,

hugging the flashlight
nearer my pillow.
Once, I even thought of you as I was being
held
and bullied after school by
several kids
who, as usual, had no reason. I

squinted harder, imagined you and it didn't hurt
me half as much. You
were all
and everything and I—the overweight,
effeminate boy
running home to read again and
rediscover

that you, at least, had not defaulted.
You, my icon,

thrown away in '83, tossed
inside the worst oblivion but not by villains
or your own depressions.
The editors said, "I'm sorry, the issues
just didn't sell."

Now, many years later, still
holding a stack
of faded, creased, and dog-eared comic books
learned verbatim, I
touch
each page like a shattering fever
and caress away dust.

AFTERNOON LOVER

You start your horrors like
engines,
caviar or cadavers, events of the heart

capsizing us all. We prolong our
moments, recline
at bedtime luxuriantly victimized—a film star

who's fallen, still waiting
for you, for
all that you offer like tip-toes in toffee,

verandahs, horizons, a spotlight
in daydreams.
You rip with vehemence right into existence

the sum of your absence. You
leave us unbridled.
We search with our hands and plunder the secret: me,

myself, my infallible image. We've loved you
like whores.
We've eaten with whispers the salt

of your fortune, now tonguing out shrapnel
still lodged
in the teeth like remnants of ardor.

A BLOWJOB

About blowjobs, let's see...
Does it lead to love
if you loiter your hands all over his body,
rise
to kiss him and again descend,
if you lick each nipple,
his shoulder, his stomach? (Well, maybe it doesn't.)
In ordinary daylight,
at least,
I've discovered that a blowjob in theory
can take away boredom,
watching
a crotch that appears to breathe with its curves
and creases,
an ebb and flow in men who approach or
stand
or sit. There's a tickle, a hiss
beneath every expression
I layer, when smiles
fall
half-off their hinges, when men disappear and potential erupts,
the eyes
move elsewhere.

WHEN YOU LEFT

Which was worse,
that my intentions leaned over and I wanted to kiss you
or that I failed to do it?
Standing too long, but not long enough
beside your car in the 2 a.m.
cold,
we witnessed our postures starving for warmth
with mirrored
      shiverings
inside of their thin layered pre-winter clothes. I fought
the urge
like a slow tug of war. My fists
which burrowed, shook down up-against the seam-corner bottoms
of each coat pocket
and then emerged—two impulsive limbs
caught coming together,
crossing the chasm
grown fatter
          between us.
I embraced your jacket like crinkling blue skin, desiring
to slither my half-warmed fingers
around your ears
and whisper confections, the liquor of truth
like an Indian summer, how
badly
    I'd dreamed

for the last two hours, stretched
side by side
in bed, watching that documentary but seeing instead
the blankets divide us,
all valleys and hills down the legs of your jeans, both hands
enfolded and
lying
across your stomach—those straight
black hairs
along the back of each wrist
    severed
by the red plaid cuffs of your long-sleeve shirt,
your Italian profile
reflecting
the colors of TV images, unshaven cheeks,

a droop of the eyelids, the tongue
at times
that would lick its lips. I was afraid to indulge, slide
elbow
       then arm
any closer together, trip us up
downhill
in a caress by accident. We spoke about nothing.

At 1:58,
that awkward habit of shoes then jackets being put back on, a
glance
at the door, an escort following you step by step
and out to the parking lot.
You needed again
my telephone number, unsure of how, exactly, the first one got lost.
We grinned
too many new grins for profit. You
told me
how you hated the weather,
unlocked your car door loudly, deliberately, confirmed
my directions back to I-95,
got in
and were gone.

HOT ASS

It's a finger, at first, that
    slides
into pleasure in search of the sweating
slow breath of taboo, an
abstract core.
A swelling of smell
among imminent moves.
It's a hot ass burning like a long afternoon. You pose,
perspiring. Your tongue
rubs sparks
against warm fallen timbers, reluctant, then wet
like a downward pivot. A day
where rain
hits
    staccato like bullets
against window blockades, shadows drip from the ceiling.
Rivers rekindle. The fabric
absorbs.

Only one "hello" and I had shed my clothes, unraveling
nude
in a fold-out bed as your hands turned over
the coals of my skin. You pause,
peripheral.
Coming in closer, a red
below
    you heating in swirls and eating the walls
out of all their whiteness.
In yellows and orange we meet
at last—
a smoldering throat, your casual match,
entwining within. A
kiss
that implodes.

SUNDAY NIGHT OUT IN THE EAST VILLAGE

There was nothing there but flesh
on fire,
swimming limbs in a sea of men. I waded in
against the current,
through arms like waves that crashed in silence, rolling in
and easing out
across
and slipping beneath my surface
over
      and
under.

A pirouette
among cocks and lava
fueling each sudden impulsive fellatio, that hairline trail
toward Mt. Vesuvius. And I was there,
like them,
erect, about to erupt
and scald the mouth of this man who has come here
to engulf the
flames.
      To smell,

then feel it,
this snail-crawling sweat down the curves of backs, moistening hair
in dank matted armpits, slithering
along
like elongating tongues. We breathed humidity,
this steam we created. Hotter
and damp
we looked around us and it fogged our vision.
We hushed our conscience, then
led the way
and like the blind we used
our hands to see.

IN BED, AT LAST

Even now, I'm unsure how you created this fire
you've set—a light in my armor of winter;
where ice endured, you have sparked desire
and shattered the cold in a flurry of splinters.
With every breath, you fog my surface,
melt the edges and burn these blues
into reds and yellows, a quick sudden bliss
of expanding orange. You lit the fuse
and conquered the darkness. I'd waited forever
for hands to warm my frozen body,
lips like yours to rub together
with mine—ignite. It is you who've thawed me,
made numbing snow into puddles of feeling,
brought summer in as December was leaving.

HOW OBVIOUS, THEN

At 5 a.m., awake and blinking, third day in a row
with a terrible headache,
I am here
in the dark of our dark blue bedroom, our
curtains shut
where morning is evening. From within your arms
and beneath the blanket
I emerge and
stumble
and bump my knee, step around the bed and
out of the door
in search of an aspirin.
It's as I'm returning that you lift your head to ask,
still half in your dream, "You ok?
What's wrong?" Like couples elsewhere,
we've learned
to speak in our own vernacular, to know that this
from you
means how much you love me.

How you say
"my boyfriend..."
when teasing my actions or
explaining my habits,
a reference to me as something of yours,
a favorite thing
kept warm in your pocket, familiar
and close; in these boxers
you bought
and then at home requested, "Try them on,"
watching me move
in smiles and longing. It's a kiss
on my shoulder
when you're half-asleep,
the doors
you open and even my hand you caress indirectly.

I come back to bed, slip in
to entangle
against your body and answer, "I have a headache.
I just took some aspirin."
Like couples elsewhere,

we all have had the same conversation. You know
that this from me,
in a disguise of diction, means
"I love you too"—
                              a reworded truth
in these early morning hours.

MICHAEL HATHAWAY

BOYS
DO NOT
HOLD HANDS

MICHAEL HATHAWAY was born in El Paso, Texas, in 1961 and raised in St. John, Kansas, where he currently lives in his childhood home with 39 cats (all spayed/neutered and vaccinated). By day he is the mild-mannered Keeper of History for Stafford County and by night he publishes *Chiron Review*, a literary journal that will celebrate its 30th anniversary in March. Since 1982, he has published more than 300 poems in various journals and anthologies as well as ten chapbooks of poetry and one of prose. Some of them are available at chironreview.com and Amazon.com.

CINNAMON MAN

the last time i saw tracy
it was spring & all six feet of him
was sprawled in a pear tree;
his brown cinnamon form
barely clothed in snug denim cutoffs.
he was smoking weed;
mutilating pear blossoms;
showering himself & me
with the shredded white remains.
from the ground i asked him
to climb down
so he could get a secret from me.
he howled like a moon-crazed werewolf;
said he was real busy
at the moment.
i knew that.
but it didn't stop my wanting him.
it didn't stop my needing
his wicked knockabout love.
it didn't stop me from nibbling
the mangled blossoms
off his dangling cinnamon feet.

ONCE WHEN I WAS SAMSON

Tom, the youngest pressman, walked into the breakroom where I was proofreading *Chiron Review* and having a Diet Pepsi. He had never spoken to me in all the time he'd worked at the print shop. He put his money into the candy machine, pushed a button and nothing happened.

His handsome, shy, young face looked perplexed and disappointed, though my eyes may have been primarily on his cute butt. Having worked at the print shop long enough to know the vending machines in the break room were more or less a gamble, he grabbed the machine to shake it, but his hands slipped off.

I looked up from the galleys of *Chiron* #32 and asked, "Machine giving you grief?"

He sighed, "Yeah, my hands are too greasy. I can't grip it to shake it loose."

I volunteered, "You want me to try?"

He said, "Yeah!"

So I stood up, faced the machine, grasped firmly and shook. Let me tell you I *rocked* that machine! I was Samson as he brought the temple down around his ankles. And Tom's heart's desire fell into the tray... PLOP!... a little bag of peanut M&Ms.

He smiled and said, "Thanks!" and took his M&Ms.

My smile flowed all over him, told him I was more pleased than he, told him of course I'd move heaven and earth anytime to please him; he doesn't even need to ask.

ME & RATBOY RUN THE GAMUT OF LITERARY LOVERS

sometimes we're jack & neal,
poking & challenging
each other's minds & histories,
entire belief systems
in motel rooms & cars
with no destinations
drunken thoughts & words roll
across the black manuscript
of strange city night skies
we move & run
as if our lives depend upon it.
sometimes i am
ginsberg & williams
& he is nameless tasty chicken.
i beg him
to let me help every inch
of his long brown body
into heaven
sometimes we are auden & kallman.
i hate him for being young.
i hate him for being in love
with the whole world.
i hate the whole world
for being in love with him.
but he is most at ease
when we are Beavis & Butt-head,
stuck in small Kansas towns
with no money,
punching each other,
biting each other,
exploring the taste of blood,
the art of pain,
creating fat purple bruises
on the canvas of our bodies.

Michael Hathaway

I'M NOT A PUNCHING BAG BUT...

he is stronger than me
and likes to hit
it is an art.
his eyes dilate,
his face gets a hard mean look,
he doubles his fist and swings wide,
brown biceps bulge
i like it,
the way it jars my whole being
that thud on my arm
or leg, or back, once in the eye
(you really do see stars)
the sheer male power behind the punch.
i never had that power,
it mystifies, eludes me.
i like seeing it, feeling it,
understanding it
i take his touch, his skin
any way he offers it

THE CLUB

when Ratboy ran off with the carnival
it hit me hard.
i was inundated with heartbroken bimbos
ringing my doorbell: where is he?!?
when is he coming home?!?
the first one cried on my shoulder,
i tried to comfort her, said,
"you know he is a wild spirit,
no one can hold him. that's partly
why we love him, why we have to let him go."
she said gently, "i know you miss him too."
she left, tears glistening down her cheeks.
the second said sarcastically,
"do *you* know where he is?
he tells *you* everything..."
i said, "yes, i know where he is.
he's flown head first
into the future embracing his destiny
with a big fat bear hug.
there's nothing you, nor I,
nor anyone else can do to stop him."
the third was hysterical,
a brain-dead, bug-eyed girl,
"where is he? where is he? oh gawd,
when is he coming home? i've been
crying for three days!!!"
i sneered,
"join the club, bitch!"
and slammed the door.

Michael Hathaway

THE PURE POETRY THAT IS RATBOY

as i unloaded the car,
Ratboy was engrossed in a tv wrestling match.
i gasped, "why don't you come here
& help me bring in the groceries?"
never taking his eyes from the tv,
he replied,
"Why don't you come here
& suck a fart out of my ass?"

LETTER TO ANITA BRYANT

This has been 20 years in the making. I was 15 through most of 1977, a Baptist by choice. Gay by birth. Not happy gay, just gay. I was smart, friendly, outgoing and talented. I wrote poems, played piano, spun records for hours on end, loved my cat Pandora to distraction, adored and respected my parents, enjoyed my friends.

Being alive was a gift. I knew that even at 15. All I wanted was for every creature that drew breath to be happy and never suffer. (I was no angel, but a Virgo/Libra child is the next best thing.)

Your face began appearing in the paper, on the news, screaming an unholy rage. I was a child and didn't understand how you could hate someone you never met.

I didn't hate you. I liked your song "Paper Roses." It was one of the records I played. I thought it was honest and cute how you stamped your little foot when you didn't win the Miss America pageant that one year.

I was 15 and didn't even know what bigotry was until you taught me. Your Christian face blowing hatred out of our tv what seemed like every night. Teaching self-hatred to children. It inspired me to dig beneath the surface of Christianity, then logically abandon it.

At 36, I understand a little because I caught myself hating back at your brick wall, slammed door face. It doesn't feel good though. I'm handing that dubious Christian gift back to you. I don't want it. I *don't* hate you, and I won't hate anyone. You can't make me.

My good parents taught two wrongs don't make a right. My hating you back won't erase the pain of inequality and discrimination.

Twenty years later, Anita Bryant, I can say this: I'm happy gay now. Being gay is my birthright. Being alive never felt better. And I love you—you paper roses, amazing grace, foot-stomping beauty queen you.

HANDS

St. John Grade School, 1972

During 3rd grade, my best friend from 1st grade-on moved to Idaho. I was devastated. A new boy moved to town from Texas: good natured, honest, a clown at heart and very real. The first time he smiled at me, my heart was his. Who knows how it started, but for two years we held hands in school every moment we were together. Until 5th grade, when Rebecca, a snotty high school teacher's aide saw us and sneered, "Boys do NOT hold hands!" She whacked our hands apart with her fist. Out of her sight, I reached for my friend's hand. He jerked it back. He walked away.

Great Bend, May, 1991

Robert and I were in the car on our first date. He was about to become my first serious lover. He reached for my right hand as I drove. I jerked away as if I'd been shot. He was hurt, and surprised as I was. I reached over, took his hand in mine. Held it the entire time I drove with the other. From then on, driving or walking, we were hand-in-hand, fingers locked against the crap of the world.

POSTCARD FROM CALIFORNIA TO MY LOVER

i woke
& remembered
there's a great
beatific world
outside
our tight hateful cocoon
it revolves
around a big fat sun,
not your dick,
& is infinitely
larger & more
generously
life-giving

Michael Hathaway

HOW TO PISS OFF A GOOD CHRISTIAN MAN

be happily gay.
live only a block away.
be friends with his teenage son.

be driving toward him on the street,
unaware his signal lights are broken.
smile and wave real big
when his hand goes up to signal a right turn.

think he is waving at you for the first time ever
after 3 years of being neighbors
like a good Christian should.

I WISH I'D MET ANTLER WHEN I WAS 13

anyboy would be cosmically lucky to spend two months
wandering the wilderness alone with Antler; exploring,
discovering the unsingable virtues of nature. learning he's been
buried under layers and layers of lies. anyboy might learn that
two boys achieving mutual joy is more manly more godly more
Christ-like than mutual annihilation. anyboy might learn to swat
Baptists like mosquitoes. anyboy might learn not to be terrified
of himself, of his ability to love. anyboy might not be eaten by
ulcers in 9th grade. anyboy might learn he was born a legitimate
child of the universe. as much as cottonwoods, buffaloes,
meadowlarks, sunflowers, as much as air, dirt, grass, stars.

MATTHEW R. LONEY

GHOSTS SPECTERS LOVERS

MATTHEW R. LONEY is a graduate of the University of Toronto's M.A. in Creative Writing program. Most recently published in India, his work has appeared in a number of North American literary journals including *Ganymede* and in the anthology *Ganymede Unfinished*. He is currently at work on a collection of short stories, *That Savage Water*, which explores the politics of third-world tourism in Southeast Asia. He lives and works in Toronto.

DRIVING TO THE CEMETERY

Wet boughs overhead scatter morning sky
        onto roads, tar skin peeled
where previous tires devastated by friction
had spun toward the gravel fringes.

Then: peripheral flash
        caught out the side window,
strobed between the sycamore trunks and thoughts
to bend the wheel into one of them,

      a mare
            flicking the paddock gate
    with her tail, hooves sheathed
    in dew snagged from the grass where
            her heels churned the mud.

Zoetropes, you'd said, mesmerize only by the illusion
        of movement—the running man or boy
losing his balloon, perpetual
tumblers in eternal somersaults—

    but are, in fact, only rapid successions of light
    eyed through alternate blacks,
    spaces littered with the rubble of living's instances.

Yet somehow, in the void
of those trunks, like gouges into
a more extraordinary universe, I keep expecting

your profile—mouth wide in laughter
or cautious lips stretching out at mine to kiss me—
to suddenly spring from that rift
back into the passenger seat, and hurdle
under this aurora of flashing sky
        together. Broken

from this circular present, that horse is there,
not you—the grave this road is leading to.

    Sun slips behind a cloud,
    its shadows robbed,
    the creature drops behind a pause of bark

>	then reappears,
>		unscathed but changed.

My god, I am trying to be certain
		that zoetropes
won't fragment everything.

>		I cannot suffer the loss
>		of yet another balloon.

TWO-BODY EXHIBIT
for S.

Around the halo of your body I've laid
the remnants of mine: Femur, radius, a rib,
a bit of skin from an unknown surface
certain to have touched you at one point

or other. These are hairs I've given you,
my hands, which I've placed directly
on top of yours. There's a kiss,
off to the side with clumsy lips
asking fish-mouthed—

there's the look I first gave you, complete
with eyelashes, a piece of iris, blue undertone
of suspicion I'm sorry
outlasts bone.

There's yesterday's argument still
stuck in my throat: "Sore
loser," it says.

Beside your sternum, like a comb,
my jawbone with molars,
pile of bloody fingertips I used

to assemble this showcase in memorium.
I've sorted all your private parts, laid
my hips onto the cradle of yours,
displayed my balls
as something left for certain,

but kept my feet,
(my right) and left
you yours.

CALENDAR WINS THE MATCH

Over the surface of the party, anxious
        like a herd too flea-bitten to settle,
        a stack of televisions broadcasts
real-time shots from the city's centre;
a transfixed, tireless multitude counts down,
as though the new year might not happen,

as though it might abandon them
        to go off with the cool kids, to disappear
        and smoke cigarettes
behind trash bins. I light a fag and step outside
in the torn coat of my aloneness.

        (Last year, it was cocaine on a plate
        through a ten baht straw—still
        in the same clothes
        as yesterday, ashamed of myself

        for having fucked
        all three of them—and the motorcycle ride back
through the oblivious, sun-ripe streets of Bangkok
to my filthy guesthouse,
        where inkblots of mould
        bloomed along the mattress seams,

        and the ceiling fan
            threatened itself a propeller
        that would unscrew from
            the ceiling to decapitate me;
        my backpack was an old
            cul de sac of memories I wished
        had the balls to disown me.)

As though when that
midnight ticks past rhythmically
        and the date is a raw bandage torn off
        the crowd behind the glass would come
face to face a blankness
that confirms what they had known
        but still hoped, for that year
            at least, to have been protected.

Matthew R. Loney

The bike driver's sweat shone in
the creases of his neck, I remember
wet accordion folds fanned
        into tiny tributaries of soil
        iron tinted red:

What a strange,
forgiving hue.

IN THE BURIED CAR

That winter the snow
covered the road and more
kept falling and fell
until the car was buried
and my breath drew itself
in frozen fishbones
on the disappearing panes.

How easily horizons change,
this new one gently rising,
like sand suffocating
the bottom lung of an hourglass.

It didn't come down to
strength or lack of
body heat, or food for that matter,
what issues you and
I had left unresolved, (the air between us
           growing staler by
the minute) hope for rescue, distant
bark of dogs, engine, snowplough, sun.

Sheer will means nothing
when at night the temperature
plummets

and the silent, pock-marked moon
lifts silvery brows over the fulcrum
of frosted window pane, curious

but disinclined
to lift a finger to save us.

DUNE-DWELLER

> *remember: space that appears to need nothing does*
> *crave, as a matter of face, an outside gaze,*
> *a criterion of emptiness—of its depth and scope.*
> *And it's only you who can do the job.*
>   – Joseph Brodsky

Asphalt tears at the wheels, as though the bike were
a bird skidding in to land on seawater roughened
by unseasonal winds, and you somewhere in a desert stuck
on the highest dune, crying that you had been abandoned when
in fact I saw you climb up there this morning with my own
eyes. Here, the jungle is carpets of vertical foliage whose buzz
transcends epiphany, where the cicadas rub themselves
into frequent, furious orgasms along the fern stems. The road
bisects the island and you scream at me from above—
Remember: space that appears to need nothing does!

Ahead of me a village, where rashes of white geese
mottle the ditch grass and a shirtless child chews a stick,
afternoon tears dried on its eyelashes like jeweled grit.
A black-haired sow spreads beside a hen coop, matrices
of anxious plumage and marble-round eyes. (Birds' feathers
weigh more than their skeletons: A crash outweighs
its collision.) So when the bike skids, the front wheel is a
traitor and a clear gasp—*fuck*—throttles my chest then drops
me down, the pavement yields only resistance. Do highways
crave, as a matter of fact, an outside gaze?

Does friction learn heat is a part of its creature? How could
space need nothing? What fills us if bones end up lighter
than feathers? You race across dune ridges with pony-tails
of sand flaring up behind you, chasing me. The child drops
its stick; a lone rev wraps the air like a turbine; those geese
are frantic white kerchiefs in diagonal vision and my hope
to outrun you is a rasped, shattered shoulder. Suffering's
in the persistence of pavement, in the drowning tide you swim
against, the eyeball revealing outer space with a telescope—
a criterion of emptiness. Of its depth and scope,

we know nothing; of the other, the façade has outweighed
its scaffold. Have I been trying to escape you, dune-dweller?
Or else fleeing to some new, unfathomable camouflage disguising
its prison as island? There you are, panting, out of breath, as the
village women run from their weaving onto the road, mocking
me. You cry—*is this thirst just a lack of oasis?*—and sob
as the children serve me lemonade from a plastic jug. We are all
kept at a distance by fears of ghosts, specters, lovers. We are all
trapped on a dune, splayed on roads, cursing—that relentless throb!—
And it's only you who can do the job.

ALONG THE SHORE

August of a past life, sepia-toned
in spectrums that register such loss
against the flashing tide pools, gull feathers,
        and our dinghy that had drifted
        to lodge itself against the water-
        snake dock like a thought
we didn't yet have the tongues to anchor.

You, slightly older, taller,
        legs glistening blond rods
picking across the shore stone until you
spy a frog, pausing as its eyeballs penetrated
the trembling moment like a spawn sac
clung for dear life to a rock ledge, those wombs
of squirming repetitions nature couldn't give
a fuck about.

        In the air, hot as lava,
        vultures crest their
        parabolas high against the timid cirrus

as the grommets of my crotch awaken;
you strip bare and wade into the lake,
        so certain, wild
        and undefeated.

IF THOSE SCALES HAD BEEN LEAVES

We'd have swum again had that mollusk's
blade not sawn your toe a mouth
that yawned then spat red smoke
      under the offshore waves and the dog
      hadn't chewed the towel or rolled
his pelt into a camouflage of grit and fish guts.

Home, to the side of the gravel road, a garter
snake flattened into a ribbon of black tubing
ruptured down the middle by
      such unbearable exiting pressure
      that it puked up its own flesh as though
death were a poison to be rid of.

If those scales had been leaves patterning
the soil with their stems or saturating you
with a punishing, chlorophyll echo,
      their roots would have hung down the
      culvert searching for a sturdier anchor
like a tail bitten off then longed for.

You could tell me how orchids aren't beautiful
parasites, that fear means looking foolish first
to ourselves or our guts are the silken
      residue of trauma when our containers
      can no longer contain them.
All this prevents you from believing that

tires aren't meant to crush but propel you?
Admitting between limps, damp
and shivering, that your father thought you a toxin
you weren't lying but were trying

      to drag your crushed and punctured body
      back into the ditch grass,

and curl beneath the tin can,
and heal completely.

THEN IT BECOMES DARKER

> *I am that angry and lonely child of always,*
> *that throws you the insult and warns you:*
> *if hypocritically you pat me on the head*
> *I would take that opportunity to steal your wallet*
>   – Reinaldo Arenas

Then it becomes darker: an airplane blinks down through
the clouds, pulling with it the sky and calls from
my mother on the opposite side of the city, her fingers
red with the insides of a cherry pie, missing me. Crouched
in the grass, the garbage is a savannah of creatures
that glint like old robots in poppy-coloured haze.
All my friends deserted me. They went to play in the ditch
—to disrupt the bullfrogs and smoke weed in the culvert.
Somehow I was forgotten, too small to retain their gaze.
I am that angry and lonely child of always

that can slip between fences, endure thirst and scraped knees,
and attacks the biggest criminal though, like a dog defending
his bitch, will still lose his fur to the teeth of the fight. Across
the street, in this neighbourhood I am lost in, two women with
black eyes pull a cart full of televisions beneath an overpass,
their plastic bracelets echoing off the concrete of Havana through
the dim-lit streets where I search the gutters for my friends.
Where did they go when the sun disappeared behind
the empty high-rise, with its crane like a sinister statue
that throws you the insult and warns you:

Boy, you are so far from home, your mother is crying
in her nightgown at the sink, her hands smoothing over
the ridges of a cabbage? And so I'll beg from you a quarter
for the camino that runs down the Playa del Este, its windows
greased by the heads of the lonely dreaming dusk children
riding home to their mothers after dark. *Get lost*, you said,
you should be out with your brother scratching paint
or pinching the wings off flies. But I'm not: I'm lost
out here, where my friends left me, wishing instead,
if hypocritically you pat me on the head

that I'd climbed into your trousers for you to carry me
clear to the continent, a stowaway—to houses with yards,
with trees, that dog mending its torn fur at the fence.
Fleas of all creatures prefer the spine, along ridges of tight bone
that can't be reached by the snap of jaws or lap of tongue.
So when I leap out, you eager to molest me, I riot
towards the gigantic black man with the snorkeling fins,
take his hand and churn up burls of jealousy you didn't know
existed. When you turn your rejected back and call me faggot,
I would take that opportunity to steal your wallet.

I'D SEEN A CONDOR
for P.

Arriving in Cuzco, the rain fell in pearls
like dark Christmas bomblets,
us wishing for jackets, so long
since shaving, some parasite caught
        from Colca Canyon where we'd hiked

down into the gorge and my boots had severed
my toenails into scraps of dangling calcium.
I'd caught a fever from the sunburn
and trembled that night with chills
until you held me like a skin and cried
into my ear a supplicant prayer
for sins you'd never bargained for.

Deserting you that morning
on the cliff side, I'd thought the trail was

       when it wasn't. I'd fumed at your fear
       of heights and pressed onward until
       the trail vanished and we had to scale the
       canyon walls, our packs full and waters empty.

Do you remember I abandoned you behind
the boulder? How the skin of my heels hung
like damp circles of paper
        and the llamas were overlords

along the puzzled paddy walls
grazing as the clouds split to unveil
that rocky citadel soaring above the
        Urubamba, threatening us?

The square was a catastrophe of peasants
camping in the rain, lighting fires, burning
crèches—one boy a gravity who tugged
at the hem of my shorts then vanished
        into the drizzle as though

Matthew R. Loney

conjured from internal nightmares. And the trek
up the hill to the guesthouse. And me shivering
in the steaming shower of broken tile work.

      And the crowds outside drunk and happy.
And you saying there was more
than one way to be brave, more than one
way to feel worthy of pleasure.

I'd seen a condor float by on an air current,
all wings and beak and updraft. Tilting
its rock-like head, we were creatures
it scanned then gazed over,
        both earthlings
        both cowards, awed by its judgment.

BROKEN BOY

I wonder at the mechanism
of my intentions as I consider whether or not
to remember you
      or to let you plummet
        back into that deep well

of memories let go of—the dying ones, dark transparent
eels tumbling into bottomless oblivion—
      almost a relief

when their screams echo cold and mossy off the stones
      then vanish—though something about
        the cylindrical space still vibrates the loss.

That memory is a choice is as certain as a grip failing
to attach itself to the dangling object.
When I toss a handful of gravel
down into that cistern, do I hear the
shock of the water attack
its own breaking surface

      or their grunting heels
        flanking you with
        bruises, hoark wads,
            relentless rape,
        shards of their bottle tweezed from
        your forehead, your torn asshole
      dripping with anger?

      (As if you had been the only broken boy,
      the only one death had ever made a valid try for.)

From my hands, the bucket drops,
the pulley gathers a frenzy of rope;

      before I even hear the splash,
      I turn and am rapt again with the forest.

JEFF MANN

ANOTHER AMERICA

JEFF MANN grew up in Covington, Virginia and Hinton, West Virginia, receiving degrees in English and forestry from West Virginia University. His poetry, fiction, and essays have appeared in many publications, including *Arts and Letters, Prairie Schooner, Shenandoah, Willow Springs, The Gay & Lesbian Review Worldwide, Crab Orchard Review, Bloom,* and *Appalachian Heritage.* He has published three award-winning poetry chapbooks, *Bliss, Mountain Fireflies,* and *Flint Shards from Sussex;* three full-length books of poetry, *Bones Washed with Wine, On the Tongue,* and *Ash: Poems from Norse Mythology;* two collections of personal essays, *Edge: Travels of an Appalachian Leather Bear* and *Binding the God: Ursine Essays from the Mountain South;* a novella, *Devoured,* included in *Masters of Midnight: Erotic Tales of the Vampire;* a novel, *Fog: A Novel of Desire and Reprisal;* a book of poetry and memoir, *Loving Mountains, Loving Men;* and a volume of short fiction, *A History of Barbed Wire,* which won a Lambda Literary Award. He teaches creative writing at Virginia Tech in Blacksburg, Virginia.

https://filebox.vt.edu/users/jemann2/

IN THE CAPITAL OF THE ENEMY

Where the bluecoats once swirled, the prostitutes festered,
whoredom became Federal Triangle. Where Sherman savored

his Grand March of victory, where Grant smoked himself
closer to throat cancer. Where Lincoln imprisoned

the Copperheads without due process or trial, signed
his Proclamation, breathed his last. This city's nothing

to a gray-beard hedonist like me but restaurants and bars.
I recommend the calamari at Raku, the grilled octopus

at Jaleo. I recommend the Green Lantern on Thursdays—
good video porn, plus shirtless boys drink free. There's

the D.C. Eagle for kink, the Motley Bar for Bear Happy Hour,
the Leather Rack for slave collars and Wiffle-ball gags.

(Aren't we Rebs supposed to be overheated and wild?
Intemperate, violent, coarse, drunken, perverse, etc.?)

Finally, I recommend an iPhone and Grindr, for then,
in between perusals of *The Wearing of the Gray*, one can

indulge in profounder urban pleasures. For instance,
this submissive Yankee with gym-fit body and graying goatee

who visits our hotel room just long enough to suck off,
efficiently, speedily, and with lip-smacking fervor,

this visiting Southerner and his partner. Soon enough
our stranger's off to the gym, never to be seen again,

and we're swilling margaritas and snarfing burritos
at Lauriol Plaza, drinking a toast to Northern hospitality.

Jeff Mann

A ROUGHED-UP REDNECK
for JW

Tonight, buzzed on cheap wine, blessed
and naked on a living room floor in Salem,
Virginia, he's licking boots into wet ebony
glisten. Now a thick knob of leather's buckled
in his mouth; now he's doubled up, bolted
steel restraints locking wrists to ankles.
His captor hangs Japanese clover clamps from
his nipples, twists and tugs the chain between
till groans well and rise like campfire smoke.
When a pair of piss-and-cum-rank briefs is
draped over his face, he snuffles the thick
scent as eagerly as a bear would a broken hive.
The boy needs to hurt, needs the heavy anchor
of helplessness, needs the reassurance
of a leather strap to unearth dull damson
bruises on his hairy pecs and back, this goateed
mountain boy drooling around his gag, sobbing
and rapt,
            and this morning, clean, so clean,
driving down back roads lined with April's
gleaming new green, purple irises, redbud
and lilacs burning on farmhouse lawns,
along the base of Hanging Rock Mountain,
where Jubal Early routed the Yanks, last
Confederate victory in the Valley, this son
of those distant Rebels, this willingly
roughed-up redneck, driving a rusting
pickup truck, CSA tattoo and aching nipples
beneath an Everlast sweatshirt, humming
and grinning to country music, pure
and light as leaves after a night's hard rain.

THE GALLANT PELHAM

> "*Stuart wept aloud over the body of his young hero–his fidus Achates.*"
> – Henry Kyd Douglas, I Rode with Stonewall

John Pelham, Jeb Stuart's artillery pet,
Fidus Achates they called him,
after Aeneas's faithful companion,
but this scene is older by far
than Rome, Latium, or Troy.
The boy has held back the Yanks
at Sharpsburg, an Alabama David
launching from his slingshot
stone after hissing stone, the boy
has broken the Feds at Fredericksburg,
damming up the blue waves, dancing
nimbly beneath their answering arcs
of cannon fire, Lee has dubbed him
the gallant Pelham, Stonewall has said,
*With a Pelham on each flank
I believe I could whip the world*, and now

like Patroclus, his body is swept
from the enemy's grasp, and now
Stuart bends over him, red beard
wet with winter and with grief,
cavalier fox tail brushing tenderly,
belatedly, the boy's beloved face, while
March snow melts on what warmth
is left in Pelham's cooling skin.
*Press forward, press forward to
glory and victory*, he shouted from
the saddle, before a flying fragment
of Federal shell shattered his head
like milkweed pod or walnut hull.
Only twenty-one years old. Stuart
cradles him, rocks him, and sobs.

Jeff Mann

Nested inside the scene, a god
does the same to a discus-maimed
beauty slowly fading into purple flower,
and a hero does the same to a hairy
wild man born of Babylonian hills,
and—so I guess—soon enough,
love, you and I will follow suit,
modern men, old men more or less,
one last caress by the sinkhole's
musty edge, the unheroic hospital bed.

A BRIEF TOUR OF McDOWELL, VIRGINIA
for Kent

> "God blessed our arms with victory at McDowell yesterday."
> — Stonewall Jackson

One by one, they pass. Stonewall's men
on Sitlington's Hill, in the new gold-green
leaves of May and the sharp stink of powder,
artillery's thunderclap, the splintered Yanks
retreating west. In the church, men in blue,
later men in gray, choking up blood, sobbing,
carving dates and initials in brick, then limping
on, if they can; remaining, if they cannot,
in the grassy graveyard across the road. Next,
the Maple Syrup Festival: crowded pancake
breakfasts, churchgoers and breeders,
the ever-fertile Southern devout, snapping
up sausage and excoriating sin. And now,
two modern mountain men, a warm day
four-wheeling through Highland County,
in the sweetest fucking Toyota Tacoma
ever built. Red goatee and black goatee,
cowboy boots and dusters, cowboy hats,
they're striding through the biannual
Battlefield Days, May breeze beard-soft
and scuffing dust from the road. They're
praising Jackson, patting gravestones, buying
syrup in a country store. They're sitting on
the truck's tailgate, sipping iced tea, gobbling
rat cheese and chicken salad sandwiches.
Soon, they'll drive deeper, down back roads,
into secret, a family cabin, a mountain cove,
the furtive exile their mingled bodies make.
Beside a trickling lick, one will kneel, suck
his buddy's cock, kiss and lick his buddy's
boots. One will strip the other, rope him
to a gleaming weeping willow, gag him
tight, beat him with a belt. But for now
both men are all they seem, happy sons
of the South, filling simple hungers
where glorious forebears once kicked
invaders' ass. For now, the sun is theirs,
the land is home, they belong entirely.

Jeff Mann

TURNER ASHBY MONUMENT, CHESTNUT RIDGE

Turner, you're hard to find, nineteenth-century
hero lost in the twenty-first-century sprawl
of Harrisonburg, Virginia. We're using
my husbear's fancy iPhone to track you,
past McDonalds and malls, aluminum-siding
housing muddle, one contemporary
abortion after another. The Daughters
have managed to save a few woods yet;
the spot where you died, bullet through
your Fauquier heart, is shaded still with
thick green oak-shade, though Chestnut
Ridge has nary a chestnut left, all brought
low by a foreign blight. There's nothing
left of you here either, save this photo on
the Civil War Trails marker. I touch
your face—onyx eyes, combed black
hair, full lips shaped for loving, the wild
dark bush of your beard. See, Turner,
more souls than I remember you. Bouquets
flank the rough stone memorial marking
where you soaked Valley earth with blood—
peony petals, areola-pink, browning along
the edges, the bright blue lupines' droop.
The Daughters, determined, indefatigable,
presiding goddesses, protectors of this grove,
horticulturalists of partisan memory, have
planted here and there hellebores, hostas,
the crimson emblems of bleeding heart.
You gasped your last in the arms of a man
who loved you *as only a fearless young soldier
can love his hero, and whose love was fully rewarded
by* your love for him, a boy who's buried
near you now in Winchester. I am too far
away to offer any warmth or comfort, but
I hope he was handsome, hope he held you
close in your damp tent those bitter winter nights,
shared with you sips of whiskey, sparse rations,
hope he gave your famous melancholy a smile,
though the wishing, like the poem, is far less about
you than me. I pluck and pocket your bleeding
heart, the sort of satiny souvenir we lovers
of knights are addicted to, lovers of bravery

and beauty who never managed to live
those things ourselves, and now John's
iPhone has found a likely lunch, and we're off
through another gauntlet of shopping malls
to Panera, though we must sadly abjure bread.
Low-carbing, we'll settle for Cobb salads instead.

Jeff Mann

AFTER THE REENACTMENT II

After the battleground's bitter cold, the conflict at Cedar Creek
fought and lost yet again, after shepherd's pie and martinis,

pumpkin cheesecake, the bushy-bearded redneck in rawhide
jacket, Stonewall Jackson cap, and lumberjack boots who

cheered the Rebs on all rainy afternoon is naked, sprawled
in a broad bed, listening to storm stroke the windows of

Winchester's Fairfield Inn. He's grinning with the perverse
pleasure of juxtaposition, to be of his region and so much not,

his husband tugging his nipples and stroking his CSA
tattoo while his husband's new boyfriend sits on his cock.

*

Allen of the smooth and loverly curvaceous butt
sleeps beside me, and John of the furry curvaceous
butt beside him. Most sweet. I'm guessing that
this is a first in history, a gay three-way following
a Civil War reenactment, but of course I'm not
the only bearded butt-pirate obsessed with the War
of Northern Aggression. I lie here beside my softly
snoring boys, and softly the rain persists, ticking
the panes like some overactive clock. Turner,
I can't sleep, thinking of you there, just across town.
The rain runs over your skull, fondles your ribcage
in Stonewall Cemetery, where you lie, Black Knight
of the Confederacy, beside the brother you could
not save. Buddy, you were just the sort I dote on:
short, dark, wiry, muscled, reckless, black beard
flowing over your breast. I would have been one
of many willing to follow you anywhere, though
partisan patriotism would have been hard-spined
with less noble motives, it is true. Adored even
after you fell at Chestnut Ridge, your sword
and spurs were stolen, relics made of your horse's
tail, your corpse's beard gone missing half a foot.
Dead like Christ at thirty-three, you would be
182 years old tonight. Damn wide ravine, bridged
only one way. Unmarried, never engaged, did

a man supposedly such an epitome of chivalry
die a virgin? Take on flesh, Turner. Slip in here,
hero, between the sheets. Let me warm you,
your back snuggled against my chest. Let black
beard and gray goatee mingle till dawn. Hairy
beauty, bravery, let me show you how a man's
body is blessed. Let me caress your torso's hard
and grassy Shenandoah hills, kiss the wound
in your blood-stained breast. Sad little brother,
Centaur of the South, teach me how to ride.

Jeff Mann

LEXINGTON BUSBOY

What are you doing here, Turner Ashby,
fourteen decades dead, Rebel hero I've come to love?
College-aged today, dressed all in black, yet I know
your jet-dark hair, the hue mine used to be, I see you
inside the thick bangs, black sideburns and goatee
of this beautiful boy bussing the table beside me,
clearing dirty glasses, forks, and plates, swift and neat
as you once swept Yankees from Virginia's Valley.
You're short and solid as before, though in this time
tattoos spill from your left sleeve, silver hoops
glint in your ears. No matter; even lovelier.
You're hirsute beneath that shirt, I can tell from here.
My hotel's near, boy. Follow me; surrender. You're
the god I strip and bind. You're rebirth rough and tender.

WEEPING FREAK

Oh, they would never have imagined you,
the Rebs who died, '61 to '65. You imagine
them, of course—compulsively. You read
and dream, you watch them shed exhausted
rank wool and step muscled and naked
into the Rappahannock and the James,
grabbing a quick bath in between battles.
You watch them panting in bloody piles
in Antietam's Bloody Lane, screaming
beneath the bone-saw in Shepherdstown.
You see a few locked together, bearded
young mouths kissing hard, hairy young
bodies spooning and furtively fucking
in shelter tents across the South. But they,
the common Confederate soldiers, men
you call your brothers, forbears, kin—really,
how many would not mock a mooncalf
so egregious? My God, man, look
at you. College-educated cocksucker,
redneck with highfalutin taste in booze,
sprawled shit-faced and naked in your bed,
left arm sleeved with swords and pentagrams,
CSA inked into your shoulder, a beard
of gray cumulus bushing down your breast,
J.E.B. Stuart style, but he died still young,
at thirty-one, don't you know this archaic
excrescence only makes you look old?
A camo cap's cocked over your face, and,
       for fuck's sake,
big hairy man that you are, half a century
old, you're crying as you read the intro
to *Stonewall Jackson's Book of Maxims*:
       "writers of every generation since
       have asserted that had he lived,
       the Confederate States of America
       might have triumphed."
       "Shit, shit!"
you sigh, wiping your wet face,
one hundred and forty-six years
after the Battle of Chancellorsville,
ridiculous how long grief and history
linger, "Shit, shit! If only...shit!"

wishing you'd been there, heroically
to leap between Stonewall and that
mad North Carolina bullet, and did they
ever find the fool who shot him? No,
and the ball opens your lung, you've
fallen at Stonewall's feet, the staunch
Presbyterian who would surely loathe
queers, he bends to comfort the scruffy
West Virginia boy who saved him, and
you're sobbing freely now, gripping
his hand, no, God no, a man such as he
could not, would not, ever imagine you.

Jeff Mann

TWO WOODSTOCK MENUS

In McDonald's, it is autumn 1991. I'm in love,
but Thomas and his husband have just moved
north, have vanished like sunlit peach petal,
windowpane frost, the mica-glitter hopes

of youth, and I am having lunch—coffee,
an unmemorable burger—with Buck,
the fay roommate they left behind,
who knows nothing of how I ache,

who—useless irony—wants me as I
do not want him. We have broken up
a drive to D.C. with this brief stop
at Woodstock, and, see, I smile and chat

as if I were still whole, as if my guts
were not untangled, strung like soldiers'
across dock and bloody stubble, as if
my body were not one hairy, lonely lie,

for from that lost lover and that long
adultery I have learned to betray
with the best, and so, embedded in
myself, I do not see, in a field nearby,

where it is May and midnight, 1862,
my Rebs feasting on stores they seized
from fleeing Yanks. They are ravenous,
the foe might be on them tomorrow,

they have everything to lose,
and so they are *determined to place
a great portion of these viands beyond
the possibility of recapture.* It's a motley
menu, to be sure: *cake and pickled lobsters,*

*cheese, canned peaches, piccolomini,
and candy, coffee, ale, and condensed milk.*
Eat up, boys, eat all you can. God knows
I did, gobbling cock-feast and armpit bush,

hairy buttocks, fur-nestled nipples, knowing
the enemy would soon arrive to rout me,
sensing what I stole would be surely stolen back.
This fate's what makes us kin: to feast, to savor

the last bite of lobster, the last bearded kiss,
and then to slowly starve. We leave Woodstock
now, you to march south, I to drive north. Different
centuries, but our futures converge. Soon we'll meet

on the same road, where empty haversacks are
dropped in mud, where youth's strength and soles
give out, where we are all brothers trudging bare
and bootless, leaving bloody footprints in the snow.

Jeff Mann

TWO LOVERS AT ANTIETAM BATTLEFIELD

I have carried this grudge for decades,
since fifth-grade history, first hearing
secession, Fort Sumter, General Lee,
Stonewall, President Davis, Appomattox.
Enthused with partisan zeal, my classmates
and I adopted nicknames among the Rebel
generals. I was Beauregard. Needless to say,
no Summers County boys—raised there
among the Southern mountains, where
the Confederate monument, in eternal
verdigris vigilance, loomed by the courthouse—
would ever side with Yanks.

                              Defeated.
Defeated. Who can forget or forgive that?
Yet here I am, standing inside Dunker Church,
strolling down Bloody Lane, with you, golden
boy, Billy Yank, son of Massachusetts,
direct descendant of Pilgrims, father from
Shrewsbury, mother from Taunton. (Exotic
New England, home of the erstwhile enemy,
home now of lobster rolls, blueberry pie,
streets where we might be somewhat safer
holding hands than in my beloved South,
foreign lands where we even might be married.)
Today we walk

                    this *veritable field of blood,*
where shy horses skirt corpse-heaps, the maimed
wriggle over earth like worms after hard rain,
night falls over cries for water and darkness
makes blue and gray indistinguishable.
A few paltry generations back, we might
have met in this field in a different, darker
manner, your Minié ball in my throat,
my Bowie knife in your gut, our limbs
intertwined in blood and mud. Instead,
I watch the rich way August light
glints your forearm hair to gold while
you indulge my eccentric and historic grief,
following my hours about the battlefield. Today
I lay down that grudge a bit, that heavy

haversack, to mourn them all, invader
and defender, Massachusetts and Virginia,
the green-sheen water under Burnside's
Bridge. With the sun, we retreat west,
as Lee's troops did, fording the Potomac,

back to Shepherdstown and the Sweet Shoppe's
marzipan-jeweled stollen, the Bavarian Inn's
gravy-topped spätzle and schnitzel. Lie close
tonight, husbear, Billy Yank, as who knows
how many furtive bluecoats and butternuts
did, despite piety and the supposed laws
of nature, in forest, tent, or smoky bivouac,
mingling beards and tongues and body hair,
blending patriotic saps, making another union,
another America.

JORY M. MICKELSON

A WEAPON OUT OF ANYTHING

JORY M. MICKELSON's work has appeared in *Free Verse, Oranges & Sardines, Knockout, New Mexico Poetry Review* and other print and online journals. He is the winner of the 2011 Academy of American Poets Prize at the University of Idaho. He's the nonfiction editor of the literary journal *5x5* (www.5x5litmag.org) and blogs about writing and queer life at *Literary Magpie*. His chapbook, *The Geography of Removal*, will be published by Winged City Chapbooks in February 2012.

jorymickelson.blogspot.com

Jory M. Mickelson

HOW TO START A FIRE
for Jessica Meade

At night, I saw you through a moth's wing
of white drapes. I was drawn to the light,
which spilled from your bedroom
into mine. I watched the yellow glow intrude.
In the window, I watched my face, a pale
flare that grows and clears at my approach.
Somehow the flesh wrong, a curious blue
the eyes, the mouth gouged out and black.

Nightheld, your wrist, the curve of your waist
in the dark, stirs a desire that rises, emerges
silently like an impossible fin and always
the swelling press against the ribs, a tenuous fist
that knuckles dumb below the solar plexus.
My breath hesitates against the glass
while you remain distant, sitting on the bed.
Your features disperse and reform, wavering
in the heat of air resisting the cool pane. I watch
until your hands put the xanthous light to sleep.

Not this night, but another when I did not watch
a fire ran its hands inside the siding of your house,
slipped quick into the window, curled on the bed to rest
before continuing to wander,
pausing to touch your belongings as it went.
It licked to flame each item in the closet,
poked into every corner of the room and stretched
until it flirted with the ceiling fan. Your house,
a drawing done in and orange and plume.

Jory M. Mickelson

GAY PRIDE PHOTO #6

The streamers and balloons have been nodding
all day in the breeze. They flutter in time
to the marching band, the drag queens strutting
the beat-thump-beat of grind-it dance music.

In the bar, it's elemental celebration: four o'clock
and you've been drinking for hours. I'm used
to the bar cupped in darkness, the August light
flooding in shows the shabby, chipped paint.

I didn't know then, you were smiling for another
camera. Everything is flashing today: the sunshine
the dance floor lights and one hundred cameras hoping
to catch the go-go boy's Speedo at just the right angle.

You still won't face my gaze. The camera predicting
what I couldn't see in this picture for months.

WHO AM I TO TELL YOU THIS?

I didn't go to the service or to the grave
nor have I spoken to your family. But I cried
about your shoes and wallet. Twice.

*

Not at the graveside, but after people argued you into chapters,
what you'd felt or thought or what you'd have to say.
Your body is better left unread.

*

O ambulance, O hospital, crime scene investigator,
O suture, O suction,
O bandages, rape kit, O coma,
O transfusion, broken appendages
O concussion, O hemorrhage,
O multiple fractures, O agonal
O contusion and blunt force trauma.

*

I hate the way they changed your story.
Shined the memory. Edited
the line.

*

Who cares if we had sex with lots of men
we wouldn't see again? Whose names
I didn't care to ask. I thought I'd remember more.
At twenty who thinks *this cock can kill?*
In between the thrusts, the furthest I got was *this cock.*

*

I still have your senior photo.
You were a kind of next-door realness.
With that blond hair, of course
you would have gotten married, served
in the military and attended church
with your adopted children.

*

It's the right thing to do.

Jory M. Mickelson

*

Beg for it.
Say, *Give it to me.*

*

It's been ten years—so long
and so many have stuffed
their writing into your mouth.
Did we actually or—
Who were you before all these others?

*

I've changed your name
to keep our conversation
recursive.

*

Do you know the difference between martyr
and misnomer, between marked
and merely?

*

Don't you want to be
an icon?

*

The last time I saw you was in a dream
of Texas, the state flag imposed upon the sky.
Lone star, what is left
between us?

*

Don't go out without me.

*

I would like to tell you things.
I would like to tell you.
I would like to.
I would.

Jory M. Mickelson

THE YEAR OF BAD FRIENDS
for James Taft

Joe Haney could make a weapon out of anything.
Give him a Bic pen and he'd hand you back a blowgun
or a spring-loaded spear. He used his darts and blades
to make us fear him. "It's your eye."

Larry Fulton followed his older brother's lead.
First the greasy rat tail, then with MGDs
and Marlboros. Finally, he started casing houses
for B&Es. "Does yer house have deadbolts?"

Clay Canby wasn't brave enough to misbehave alone.
He needed Larry or another boy to lead the way
into trouble like two trestles of some perilous train,
always asking, "So what's the plan?"

Henry Janek was the tallest boy in three grades.
Rarely without his drumstick in motion, tap-tap-
swack on the back of the bus. His pale face against
green vinyl. He didn't have much to say.

Mike Hoyle had a home-cut mullet and dark straight bangs.
He introduced me to Def Leppard and how to "borrow"
a car. Made his money killing gophers in the neighbor's
fields. Saying, "I hate it when they squeak."

*

Not too far south of here
there's an old Indian tree,
some kind of pine that's
s'posed to be holy.

Their coyote god was causin'
trouble, turned into a ram
and ran into it, the horns stuck
and the head locked in.

So I don't know if coyote got eaten
by the tree or what, but even now
Indians still tie ribbons to it,
red and yellow in the wind.
So we borrowed Martin's

folks' car. Too scared to drink
the beer that Larry brought,
I swallowed my fear instead.

*

Sometimes when I sleep I dream
about the old blue Ford we stole,
about being twelve and running,
about bravado and ram heads,
and climbing ribbons of smoke.

Sometimes when I sleep, I dream
about dozens of dark cars orange with fire,
about Joe Haney's axe shining until I'm blind,
about horn white teeth stained black with blood,
and always the rising blue sail the wind.

*

"Only pussies wear seatbelts," Henry finally speaks.
"Don't be a dick," Larry says, "Have a drink."
"C'mon faggot, take a swing," says Mike and Clay.
"If you don't," Joe says, "I'll stab you."

*

I split that trunk with a hundred
hard swings, we all did, taking turns.
The ribbons too high to reach,
even for boys who clamber to the top
of apple trees. Swack-swack-swack
the axe bit into the wood, sometimes
sticking fast as the head of a ram.
Drunk, we let coyote out for good.

*

Going home, a coyote crosses the road in front of the headlights
like boys leaving footprints on the bottom of a pool.

IN ANTICIPATION OF WINTER

Janet, Doug and I dig through the soft-cornered boxes labeled
winter in dark marker. We've been watching the weatherman's
radiating drape of lines come down from Canada. An arctic
front fingers south and so we spade the layers of green
and grey sweaters, exhume the crooked roots of gloves.

It's Doug who raises the dull blue scarf, suspends
it across his arms. One end cascades back into the box,
a cold reminder that Steve isn't with us. But Doug
doesn't know. Janet's mouth, her eyes, Steve's memory.

A year ago: the late night calls, the can I stays, the I'm on
my way just leave nows. I take the scarf, fold it away.
Janet's standing, headed to the kitchen. Out the window,
against the streetlights I see the first snow fall.

Jory M. Mickelson

I CAN'T REMEMBER THE OTHER STORIES
for J.W.B.

Sometimes I watch *Ghost Hunters*, where an unshaven man
with tattoos tries to get through to the other side. EVP, electronic
voice phenomena: ask questions into the air, pause, ask again.
Nothing whispered in the ear, but when the tape's rewound,
there are voices, audible almost.

Days later I catch myself leaning into the static between radio stations,
whispering at the white hiss. Can you hear me? Are you there?
But I can't play it back to be sure.

I've been reading about the history of Spiritualism,
the Fox Sisters were the first to hear walls tap, make tables
rap. They were tied into chairs, and still cracked their joints
like chicken bones, claiming the spirits were among us.

Last night I had a dream that you call me,
half way through the conversation I realize you're
dead. Laughter glowing through the line, you say,
"Of course I am. Where do you think I'm calling from?"

Jory M. Mickelson

FLIGHT PATTERNS
for Will Seward

You will know this bar by its studied
anonymity. You can watch us
migrate through this town by year,
by bar, by visible rise and fall.

When too many birds gather on a fence line
a farmer fills his gun with shells.
Whispers coalesce into scorn;
police begin to frequent the streets,
prices double, drinks get weak.

I know the history of flight back to The Flame,
its giant neon torch that wicked the sky,
high booths and decorative drinks—
still-life with homosexual and daiquiris.

Where we gather, locals once called "the Pit,"
replete with concrete stalactites,
caged dancers and a rock waterfall.
It's called the American Veterans' Bar, now.

Let me tell you how to enter:
Don't stop. Don't respond to people
on the street. Go down the stairs
and through the door. Stay out of sight.

And if the police arrive, watch the scattershot
of wings as we take flight.

WHEN NOT A SONG

The birds' bills as quick
as Singer needles
sidle against the
slick estuary mud.
Their feeding makes
a villainous *click,*
click, click. Brown heads
stretch the whole body
forward leaving a
ribbonous track down
to the saltwater. When
eating the Gadwall
is nearly silent.
They do not call,
but whistle low
and the beating
of another's wings
will drown out the small
and thinner sound
of a duck's hello.

ERIK SCHUCKERS

The Light We Swallow

ERIK SCHUCKERS lives and works in a 97-year-old house in Pittsburgh, Pennsylvania. He studied literature and writing at Allegheny College and the University of Sheffield. Before finding a niche in the nonprofit world, he worked as a bookseller in the United States and in Brighton, England.

erikschuckers.wordpress.com

INDULGENCE

Rain in the city: the boys move
through the streets like surfers on a wave
of dark neon, sculpted in the lathe
of cruising headlights.

On Ian's boots: the gleam
of nameless tongues. He wears a crewcut
swastika in which he fails to believe, a knife
in which he does not.
                        His lover is a punk stitched
tight with safety pins and scars, so thin
he's nicknamed Angel, shoulder-
blades like wings.

Behind the station, a hipster Ziggy
Stardust twink, tangled up in hair and shadow,
bows in iron half-light.
                      Sheltered by the skip,
David shimmies down his drainpipe
jeans, becomes another son.

In these rented alleys where
crumpled bills are borne like votives
in cupped hands, where whispers in stained
toilet stalls buy penance with a ten, you learn
to taste the silver on men's tongues.

Out here, you know
    where you stand
        where you kneel
            and how

you can pay for this innocence.

Erik Schuckers

CARNIVAL LOVE
from a line by Tom Waits

But crank up some of that old sideshow shuffle
on the phonograph and dance, and doesn't the creaking
of the floorboards almost sound like the Himalaya minutes
before it flew to bits in Cairo, Illinois, spraying rotten
wood and rusty cogs into the crowd?

And wasn't there a witness, a kid round-
bottomed as a kettledrum? He loitered near the ghost
train while you busied yourself with the novel you'd brought,
in case the games proved (as usual) hopelessly rigged,
the eight-fingered carny immune to your charms.

Madame Stolichnaya told you nothing
you couldn't guess, if the voices would leave you alone.
Her accent fled Budapest for Baltimore. You couldn't pay,
but you let her stroke your thigh as she passed out,
staining the Minor Arcana with Max Factor.

You passed the twins behind the midway.
Later, they'd narrate your face in turns: this one
the veins of your eyes, that one the chop of your brow.
When it was done, the sketch was unrecognizable.
Copies flap forgotten across the midwest.

But that was years ago. The carnival winters
in hurricane country: like us, not much to look
at anymore. You think I'm going to sing like a canary?
This throat's as tuneless as the whistles of a steam
calliope gone cancerous with rust.

Stake me one more time inside
these canvas alleys with a hallelujah and a hard-on.
Resolve, like wood, softens with age. And I wish
I had some whiskey and a gun, my dear.
Some whiskey and a gun, and you.

AUBADE FOR A CLOSET CASE

The storm that comes
at night is gone by morning.
What's left behind as evidence
   (grass ambiguously wet, spill
       of earthworms, split tree)
stir us rich with absence:
   the phantom scent of lightning,
       ghosts of clouds rolled thick with rain
          (a tonic that transforms
             but does not remedy, which leaves
                the soil slaked and thirsty, as it was,
                   which leaves a fretful silence.)
This spider's clutch of hair. This wrinkled
sheet. A spreading damp.

Erik Schuckers

REQUIEM FOR A JOCK
from Rec Rooms of My Youth

The cash ran out before
your father did, and so the room remains
an implication. Beadboard panels slack behind
the water heater, scoliotic, while a nubbined
couch exhales Salem Lights and grease
across an archipelago of shag burnt
bitter orange. The VCR plays
Nightmare on Elm Street, a copy you boosted
after school, your cousin's shift, his clerk's
mustache a pubic squib, as insubstantial
as the men who drive your mother to
your JV games. In the living
room upstairs, women sit in lawn chairs
drinking Schlitz, an afternoon as full of holes
as the bathing caps through which their frosted tips
are tendriled, the stink of hair peroxide hot.
Onscreen, the jock has been locked
up, wrongly accused of his girlfriend's murder,
but what would you think of his story, what
would anyone: a body scored
by unseen razors, harrowed flesh
tilling itself in the indigo hours of a small-
town bedroom? You tell me your dad moved
to Wyoming. (Florida last year. Before, we both
forget.) Because you want me
to, I try to picture cattle, widescreen skies,
telephone calls, but in my head, Wyoming is
metallic, humming spaceship gray, horizon flat
as a power line. It has nothing
to do with the animal heft of your forearm,
or the way you wrestle me to the floor, scissored
in the humid V of denim, your sweat less scent
than flavor: tomato soup and copper pennies.

Erik Schuckers

As Ronee Blakely scuffs drunk-eyed
to the cellar to reveal the backstory, the only
part she believes, the part that ends in revenge
and furnaces, you get up for a piss.
Sometimes you sleep down here. I've found
a gray-heeled sock behind these cushions, a stained
tee shirt, once a book, a Hardy Boys we're both
too old for. I lower my face to the rough
plaid. Outside, the light's a bruise
that no one can remember raising, hairdo
weather fading faster than a pair of dusty taillights,
Florida weather. Johnny Depp is sucked
into his bed, erupts in a geyser
of blood, and twenty years later, you're seventeen
years gone, unshuttered as a summer
Saturday, an incomplete pass spiraling too
blue, too bright for memory.

Erik Schuckers

LEVITATION

In the raw space that opens up between
the touch and its memory, and in the margins
of letters crossed by foreign suns, we have moved
like spies through our winters.

The codes that we invented
to speak across the frozen warp of these
geographies no longer do, not here, where finally
no passwords work: the border gate has gone,
and only darkness fingers through the slats
of this deserted outpost bar.

We inked each other's histories
and myths on every ragged scrap of skin,
but we were younger then, and leaner, balancing
angels on a fingertip, fragrant with spring
mud and unspilled cum.
                        Now we travel
like gypsies, snow magicians, to another country
stretched ice-sharp beneath an Arctic moon.
Nothing has prepared us for our lives.
We cross the bridge that spans the noiseless river,
and our bodies hang fire in the night.

Warm brother, let us burn
the old communiqués, as out of date
as Russian maps, and let our tongues forget
the words we learned, the clichés as easy as the men
we became. We may discover in our silence
the language that will save our lives.

CROTCH SHOT
for Brian

There's always an SUV
in the picture: alighting, departing, the traffic
of boldface names and bodyguards, the douchebag
in the driver's seat.

Tomorrow's late night dig tonight
is one abstracted moment juggling the cell
phone and the Johnny Rockets blitzed, or else
a calculated risk, tabloid bank and grist for milquetoast
twinset scolds of MomTV, and those old legionnaires
of virtue whose skin puckers like stale bologna,
an easy target framed
by lunar thighs and a raveling hem.

Across LA, rows of car doors pop
like Rockettes' knees, deliver us a line of shaven
schadenfreude: vacant heiresses fragrant with pink
tragedy, rehabbed starlets limned in nightclub
glitter and night-vision green, teen divas
from the early aughts whose reinventions stalled
in indie hookerville or *Lifetime* limbo.

Blame it on their parents,
or the paparazzi. Cluck hairy tongues
and Google the hacks who giggle and preen, tiaraed
toddlers in a pageant we've agreed to fix. Cast stony
votes of outrage toll-free or by text, standard
rates apply:
            mindless that we're all one tender
shot away, galloping pantsless into the fish-
eye lens and flashbulb morning.

Erik Schuckers

THE FACE OF GOD IN JOHNNY WEIR'S ASS

If your ass were a missionary, it would wear
black-and-grey pinstriped Spandex, linger in suburban
doorways, troubling the faith of home-based marketing
consultants and middle-aged jocks, inspire at last
its own kink, latex, Xtube fans.

If your ass were Kirk Cameron, the Seaver family's
dominance among the neighborhood would be uneasy,
hard-bellied sons chambered at twilight, laugh-track
hours stuttering, mattresses too thin against
the growing pain of adolescent bones.

>   *Confession*: In my youth, the seminal
>   family sitcoms featured boys with elegant
>   lines, voices soft as polo shirts, assembled cheek
>   by limb from *Tiger Beat*, lithe readings of a single
>   script, blond Burbank Tadzios who'd smell like
>   swimming pools and Prell. I slopped on summer
>   beaches like a porpoise sausaged into Sears swim
>   trunks, chubster tits asweat, nipples purpled
>   woozy sunbursts, stomach soft enough
>   to land a joke, or punch.

>   By the time I saw you skate *The Swan*,
>   I'd slept with every man who asked.

If your ass had been filmed by Cecil B. DeMille
for the kind of Biblical epic that no one makes these
days, it would have undermined the lead with such supple
ambiguity that decades on, it would remain
the only wholly glorious performance.

If your ass were filmed by Lars von Trier, bare
light bulbs noosed above the soundstage would conspire
in forgiveness, even as unspeakable events befell
it, like being kissed by Udo Kier or married
to Chloe Sevigny or sung to by Bjork.

>   *Confession*: Hungry, I'll swallow
>   anything, even grace. Hungry, I'm crawling
>   bad intent and coprolalia, scars and cigarettes.
>   Hungry, I commandeer this crewed
>   skeleton, skein of bones in jukebox denim,

whistling misfortune like a tune. And if hunger
were enough, you could sharpen a skate
on my rib, a line on my tongue, send me down
the runway like a trick of neon and vodka,
sequined spider-webs and vacant lots.

Fallen Angel: you devour the cameras like crushed
ice. Yielding, I jack off twice and fall asleep.

If your ass were Lisa Whelchel, Blair would be
the succulent offspring of a Russian count, surveilled
by Frau Garrett, Germanic heft and iron box, through corridors
of savage wallpaper, uncovering the facts of life in
basements strung with razor wire and fairy lights.

If your ass were a televangelist, all I have to offer—
perilous house, a wardrobe hung with dubious judgment,
camera-ready thighs and failing knees—I could not surrender
fast enough to redeem these tornado alley years, static with
catastrophe, deaf as rainclouds, dumb as a double-wide.

Erik Schuckers

TWO EDINBURGH SONGS

1. Royal Mile

Your city, not mine.
We have come without you—
one who's never known
you, one who has
> has loved you twenty years
> since August sun turned angles
> on the water where we swam

—and we have walked
the Royal Mile, summer prince,
from the Castle past the old stone close
to the Palace of Holyroodhouse.

And we have seen
your city abandoned in the spring
and heard your voices singing
to us songs we could
not understand
but hold
as water holds the cool stones
dark below the current.

> Sea-swimmer, heir of tide
> and crest, we steer by this scythe
> moon, sharp and clear as the memory
> of your breast when we were young.

2. Arthur's Seat

We have climbed here
in the early morning where
the gorse grows thick and sweet,
and the city spreads beneath
us: wings from fire.

Halfway up, loam-stained
in the arch of the ruined chapel, we
stand to watch the swans alone
on St. Margaret's Loch.

 And you are the bread they swallow.

I've cultivated myth in
sun and sleeplessness, false
memory and fine whiskey, turned myself
a history from what we didn't say,
the sorrowful freight of youth.

I've crowned you king
of unrecorded prophecy, filled
the sky with your sweat and cum
and drunk the rain.

 And you are the light we swallow.

Erik Schuckers

VARIETIES OF AUTUMN LIGHT

The wind through these dry leaves
a kind of faith, this season of redemption granted
far from spring's apology, its wassail sun our water,
our wine. It all comes down to this.

And the hollow of your throat,
the curve of your stomach, the gentle arc
of your cock: these too save. In autumn country,
we build fire in the cave our sleeping bodies make,
our dreams a dark illumination shifting
shadows on cold stone.

I love the ache of these
October mornings, the shiver
of the ax through knotted wood. How reluctantly
you wake in this sea-light, the weave of you against
my skin, and turn to me the last unbroken
thing in this season of passing,
this provisional grace.

To know that we are leaving,
irrevocably, and discover in the slant of dawn that strips
the night's horizon: this is enough.
This is more than enough.

Erik Schuckers

THE WARRIOR IS LEARNING HOW TO FIGHT

> *The master's tools will never dismantle the master's house.*
> *– Audre Lorde*

Chill of kitchen tile slick
with steam, spaghetti boiling soft
and Liebfraumilch on ice.
Outside,

December breathes exhaust
and snow while here, in the borrowed
intimacy of someone else's flat,
the simmer of our bodies rolls
fog against cold windows.

We cannot even see the dark.

You move to clear
the glass I want to shatter,
long to pass through free to wind
and shadow, and in the sudden
muddy mirror of its face
we stand revealed:

two men moving
toward each other, pouring candle-
light from hands which have made war
and bread, which have set fires
and tables.

In the crazy flicker
of our light, I can see
the pane bending.

KAT SMALLEY

AWFUL BEAUTIFUL TRUTH

KAT SMALLEY is an undergraduate at the Florida State University, where she is pursuing a double degree in Creative Writing and Philosophy, as well as transitioning to womanhood. She currently lives in the city of Tallahassee.

Kat Smalley

THE BOY ON THE BUS WHOSE JUNK
I FELT UP, MIDDLE SCHOOL

I remember one instant,
like seeing water clearing,
and the boat of my heart becoming reeds,
gliding across blue lotuses.
It was the last day of classes,
and we were sitting next to each other
on the bus. You were your
brother's twin, though easy to distinguish,
you shared the same hair color—
the white-yellow of Dominican amber,
the same fleshy lips that bend languidly,
the same eyes that fall half-lidded
colored like some undiscovered emerald
carved out of Colombia's hidden latitudes.
Your face, though, was skinnier,
cheekbones traceable, personality
more delicate and more amused.
I can't remember the conversation that
led up to what would happen;
I was too caught up in the thought
of feeling every part of you
naked, against the pleather of the
seat. I put my hand on your thigh and
grinned like an adolescent cat,
hungry from the smell of you,
backpack draped across our shared laps,
leaving our explorations
to ourselves and stranding us on a sandbar
of desire on that moving bus.
I bit my lip and rubbed. You said
nothing, but I saw that silent sign of your
approval pressing firm against the denim
of your jeans, encouraging the first moment
I realized that I was gay.
The moment when I realized that I would
rather be with you, fingers in the thatch
of your blond pubic hair, in that awkward
adoration of you and maybe more importantly,
your cock,
the moment when I am trapped in fear,
the good fear, of discovering awful, beautiful truth,

like a fire-worshipper in his temple,
who sacrifices tight bundles of fresh mulberry
branches to the frenzied bonfire
and burns his fingers—
this is what your body means to me.
This is what you mean to me.
With some sudden courage, I slipped
my hand into your burning bush,
fingers ringing around your tumid
trunk, its body throbbing with desire
that matched my eyes and hands.
I came out unscathed, except
by the desire to be with you,
along you, underneath you, to be
pathetically in love with you.
The bus stopped, and
I had to sit there, desperate for—
well, desperate for you all night long.
You got off the bus with your twin,
your callipygian butt dancing
away, and I would never see it again.
The boat flowed down the river.

ABOUT YOU IN NEW YORK

I think about you—
pretty blond faggot in a blue
shirt, hair stylish,
stud peeking jauntily from one lip's corner,
wandering through the bookstore.

And I think about
the Metropolitan Museum of Art—
shattered bronzes,
and a marble guy who
looks like you, lips parted
as come-hitherish and plump as yours.
He is missing an arm
and his lips look hurt instead
of slyly confused like yours.

So when the sun sets between
two towers like a garnet in
a Celtic altar, it will
never set that clean again.
And New York City, too,
will sink into the Hudson
like the ancient brownstones
of Alexandria.

And least of all, you,
pretty blond faggot,
will evaporate like the brunch-time
talk of socialites.

And I think about the Mayans—
disappeared, devoured, who left,
maybe out of love,
masks of beautiful faces all in jade
and I am suddenly struck
with the desire
for someone to sculpt in jade,
or marble, the entirety of you,

so when everything is gone, and
future worlds are digging up
our vulgarities and desolation,
they will find you under dry water.

They will not think of us
as lost, but think of us
as you.

MR. PAUL V., ELEMENTARY SCHOOL

I never liked you.
You were too pretty, too self-aware of that fact,
too charming and well-loved and blond,
too willing to be a sort of casually cruel—
backhanded cruel, the kind of witty savagery
that only men like you can do,
with cold blue Aryan eyes and pointed Frankreich features.
Ach du, mein Lehrer, nein, mein König.

But then, you taught us Shakespeare,
showed us Zeffirelli's Hamlet, sitting in the dark to watch,
your eyes becoming pale and almost tearing up
when the Dane-Prince gave his riddle,
as if "to be" for you was much more painful than
"not to be."

And when you assigned us to act out the play
and made me Hamlet,
I wanted to break your heart
when I stood up on stage, reciting from the text:
"What a piece of work is man!"

You killed her.
The first-grade teacher you had taken
to a motel,
you shot her in the skull and then
you shot yourself.
They had lied to us, told us you had died
on a snowmobile.
A girl wept, another gasped.
When I found out the truth, I didn't tell
a single soul,
and I wished I hadn't known myself.

Oh, what a piece of work is man.

UNBURIED BODY

The bog body, Windeby I

Delicate boy,
they must have suffered from love of you.
You who have wandered
through white birch boughs,
long arms as white as yours.
They must have had words,
the men, for you:
Unser kleines Stutenfohlen,
things said only with their
bitten tongues and eyes.
We'd have different names,
like faggot.
Long hair of cream-color
held well in hands. Your body,
breastless, hairless,
everything sublime
like floods surging
through the banks,
more dangerous than
mere spears or war, or
even women.
And they'd have known
what makes them weak.
It's no surprise.
He must have taken you in the night,
in the smell of straw and sweat,
big dark Svaðilfari inside of you.
Love makes you cruel.
They busted out your arms,
and all those men
with fearful eyes like deer
held you under water,
birches on your chest.
Before they did, though,
one of them
took your hair
and pulled it back,
keeping it out of your eyes
with a soft hand-knitted headband.

FRANKENSTEIN AGONISTES
for Evan J. Peterson

The Jew or Nazi had created me,
golem or an Aryan,
idol of a God who does not come.
From wire and lightning,
the stolen cunt and womb
of a Congo slave
rumored to have worn a knotted leopard's skin,
I rise,
cow's tongue dully scraping out
        "I will lay sinews on you, and will cause
flesh to come upon you."
Doberman muscle,
ushabti steel-wired to my sternum,
Herr Doktor germinating
his own image inside of me
in the charnel house of Ingolstadt.
Herr Doktor's dead now,
and his black heart, with one quarter
bitten out,
is lying on my mantelpiece.
His monster has rejected him
in favor of
the taste of boys
and image of the girls of the discotheque.
You could say
my *own* heart remembers
in its own way—
each pig-valve fibrillation
telling you my story.
Listen, liebling,
lump of organ meat.
It could tell you
what you wouldn't believe from me.
I am a process, not a noun,
I am Herr Doktor's
hating and his loving
given dead children's
milk teeth—
from a girl, from a boy.
My own organs all remember,
and they will be beautiful.

Call me the Kalos,
stitched-up Galatea,
call me the nightmare
made from dog
and man
and eye of newt and
woman-sex,
call me
        (on the line, call me,
call me any day or night).
And if you'd like
I'll take you home.
I'll show you a black and
withered heart,
my stitches.
Promise not to scream
if you find my hands inside you, my love,
my skin,
my heart, and oh:
my womb.

DAVID-GLEN SMITH

Burn Down All Bridges

DAVID-GLEN SMITH lives in Cypress, Texas, with his partner of ten years and teaches English Literature at both Wharton County Junior College and Lone Star College—CyFair. He received his M.F.A. at Vermont College, and his M.A. at the University of Missouri at St. Louis. Currently, and most importantly, he and his partner have welcomed a baby boy into their lives. Smith's work has appeared in various magazines, most recently: *Q-Review*, *ffrfr*, *Saltwater Quarterly*, *Houston Literary Review*, *Lady Jane Miscellany*, *Slant*, *Ganymede Unfinished*, and *The Write Room*.

davidglensmith.blogspot.com

I TELL MY SON TO BURN DOWN ALL BRIDGES
for Brendan

Without hesitation,
shove kindling and kerosene-soaked-rags
under the foundations of any structure
binding your slender body to the past,
incinerate the litany of misguided perceptions,
broken advice, miscalculated directions
which led you down dead-end gravel roads
at dusk, where even technology fails
to establish a connection to your self-worth,
self validation.
Without regret, fulminate,
strike bundles of matches, cup the small flames close,
and shield the fever against your chest,
then light all combustible materials within reach,
the cracked plywood planks
built across the river of your life—
fuel the developing fox fires
with tinder and last year's seasoned branches—
collect brushwood to throw into the pyre
with glorious affirmation.
Without looking back,
acknowledge the ash which rains down as soft snow
and the sheets of fire which expand, licking up
further beyond any flash point. Encourage the blaze,
to vesicate, sear lumber and stone—
without turning, you must visualize the heat
at your back, blistering the nape of your neck,
singing the tips of your coal black hair, and then,
only then, step away. Motion forward—keeping your eyes
centered to the cool darkness ahead.

David-Glen Smith

METAMORPHOSIS: ODE TO AN OLYMPIC DIVER

There are times when you appear, without warning,
    deus ex machina, your figure as an angel
        walking along the arches of heaven
before the dive, the moment
    of hesitation, a precise time
        before translation, before your actions
            of folded arms and legs, and wings
    emerge from the angles of bone and flesh—
change into origami papers: Japanese cranes
    leaping out towards the moon—
or pale marsh egrets flashing their wings in wide arcs
    open to the night sky—
but I am not a sculptor, I am a poet.
    My body was fashioned to stand motionless,
        withdrawn, a gray-brown fedora on my head,
cloaked in a long, winter coat. Only
    my hands were made to move,
        puppets, marionettes dancing across paper,
            accenting phrases when I talk aloud,
    even to myself, or in my sleep, my fingers tapping,
knotting themselves in nervous positions.
    Even at this moment, trying to motion myself
into this verse, my hands become agitated with me,
        angry that their only function

is to raise an apple to my lips, serve as figures
    of transportation from plate
        to mouth. They want more out of life,
to create words flowing, a new text,
    or to recreate your figure in clay,
        knead life into the earth, raise
            a motion into your elevated limbs,
    a figure in motion, animated life poised above me.
Sometimes, posing before mirrors, I stand naked,
    worry about the pale conditions of my body:
it will never know you, but then, in the gymnasiums,
    I push to transform my image,
to move towards a higher function,
    to be more than just a word-smith
        breathing words into the ears of the public,

syllables across the eyes of librarians. Do you hesitate
    before the fall? Do you dream as a bird?
        I've been told when a young swift
           travels across western Europe,
      it motions through instinct only,
  never landing, never ceasing to be
    anything *other* than a mere vehicle of flight, of wings.
It feeds on insects in the air, sleeps in higher altitudes on drafts,
    currents of high winds. It knows not how to fall
I once wondered of these motions
      of the insistence of gravity's pull back to earth

or my persistent nightmares of my father, scenes with his doppelganger
    dropping my brother into a well, or a bottomless cavern.
      Dark, unbidden thoughts of children.
If I try, I recreate the fear inside my chest;
  the same fear when I took the first fall
      into deeper Gulf waters, learning to swim, my father
      behind me,
    invisible to the trauma. His insistence
  to submerge me I could not understand—but my brother,
I kept trying to make him grow wings, against his falling,
  to raise him back into waiting arms,
return him back to the folding of security, into a warmth,
  body no longer held by water, but by parental strengths.
Swimming for me now is different.
  There no longer exists a curiosity
      of the loss in gravity. Swimming now
is effortless in a sense, merely a means to be alone,
  floating, almost motionless. The old fears,
    and the memories, return at this time,
again unbidden, but as an adult I've learned
  to shut them off. Close the eyes tighter and
cast them away as stones, into the bottom
  of the tides. I remain, as yourself, poised above,
hands reaching out for something unseen, as a stolen Greek statue,
  glorious and defiant in fragmentation.

METAMORPHOSIS: ODE TO KENNY FRIES

I want to hold you
        in my camera, preserve the quiet nature
                of this scene, of you sleeping, the bed sheets
pulled up from around you, wings opening,
        yourself lying as Hephaestus resting,
                muscles still taunt from smithing new armors.
                      When I tried holding you that summer,
        you spilled from my hands, a fountain,
an overflowing of words; you could not even
        fit in my mouth, your language filling me
entire, choking me with poetry,
                with masculinity as I read verses aloud,

your voice slipping from my lips,
        possessing my tongue with your texts.
                When we kissed, a slight taste
of salt lingered, the ocean intent on staying,
        remaining with us, even at nightfall
                with the soft lowering of your clothes,
                      a lowering of the tides. This is the same day
        your landlord tore out of the earth the old oak in the backyard;
noise from the saws ran along the cape all afternoon, into the night,
        ripping across the white beach houses, the narrow streets,
reaching the men in the dance bars dancing slowly in pairs.
                Your body remained heavy with the afternoon.

I still remember your sweet weight over me,
        sand lingering secretly on your skin, in your scalp.
                And with the morning sun, the sheets spread out,
from your upper spine, exposed portions of your body to me,
        exposed the back that supported my love-making.
                A horse neighed in the distance.
                The sun blazed up higher,
        exposing you as the god of metal-work,
the god that broke my name under his hammer
        creating *myths* out of *smith*, the god with bird-like bones,
a god I cannot encompass,
        with my human hands.

METAMORPHOSIS

The moon was not even aware of him,
of the boy climbing the water tower,
      a figure held against the graffiti
            and a rising tempo of the moment.

The boy was suspended above time. Above
the town. And though the moon did not watch him,
      he watched the moon. The slow rowing across
            still water. At the top of the tower

he paused, opened his arms as if to take
in the silent crescent on the horizon,
      or even the town itself, as if one
            could embrace rejection. In a sense

he became the moon, a paleness spreading
his arms—or rather, he opened them
      as a memory, as my memory,
            of the time I was 17 and knew

I was different, but could not name it;
only felt the presence here, in my chest,
      a rhythm beating at night, as I tried
            to conform my thoughts to what I was told,

what I was taught. The drumming never ceased.
It grew, over the months and years, became
      a persistent hum in my ears, my throat
            breathing with the motion, until I saw

myself for what I was: a pale changeling,
my form metamorphosed to a bird,
      soft feathers covered my hands and shoulders,
            a soft down of my new self surrounding

my form like a warm coat, a strong embrace
of acceptance; the kind I wish for this boy,
      for this scene of the boy alone. He breathes
            in the moment; his blue hour tightens.

He arches his back and falls forward,
into the arms of emptiness, of night.
    Can you imagine such a falling?
        The denial of the self arching the body,

casting it into a death of scandals.
I used to stand on rooftops, on houses
    to feel the moment of it all, to try
        and abandon myself into the wind.

But I realize now, I am like Horace,
an old man chasing young girls and servants,
    all for the sensations of past flights
        of fancy, a man picturing himself

with wings, an old crow tonguing the moon
with songs of beauty in a passing face,
    the hard-hearted boys that tempted him
        with their hard bodies, their rough sports.

My wings cannot take me backwards in time,
to change events swallowed by history.
    I hover softly in the present times,
        cursing my lack of angelic powers,

wanting to will myself to the falling,
hold back the events. To re-cast the boy's form
    into a new image, if only into the shape of a passing swallow,
        or a young swan shifting eastward—by night.

LISTEN
for Lowell

Listen, close. You can hear the pale subtle
opening of the magnolia blossoms
willing out their voices in St. Louis.
Euclid Avenue darkens with their heavy,
lifting mouths, their burning with memory,
low murmurs of your voice absent now from cafés—

And there was a time I meant to tell you more,
how you unfurled in me aspects I once thought
were lost, portions that made up my whole
voice—as a whisper in Spanish: *nadamos
en los ojos de dios* or *tus manos*
language made liquid to echo the flow
of your warm gestures, your fluid words. *Listen*,
as memories of you fall from my pen.

David-Glen Smith

AN UNTITLED POEM FOR BETH

Did this time ever really exist?

I mean this scene, of you
and I in a small, dive bar,
lost alongside the river front, where the ghosts
of the past wander among the living,
not as I once thought—out of loneliness—
but as a means of remembering themselves.

Only I seem able to see them tonight,
lost in the renovations, the reconstructions founded
to house local bands, joints patronized by women
with too bright make-up, neon lips, dark eye shadow,
and men who tie their unwashed hair back in a long,
slender tail.

Honestly I am trying to avoid the past,
as much as I am trying to avoid this present, ignore
the eyes of the dead, as they casually touch
a shoulder, kiss an upturned face.
Unseen, they stroke us, watch the patterns
we dance on the wooden floors. They watch me,

as I try relating to the irony of you dancing with me, two friends
with a music heavy in bass, electric sequences,
and an off tempo drummer.
                                      I feel out of place,
almost a ghost myself trying to pass as someone else,
a ghost of a fox perhaps, wearing the awkward guise

of human form, the disguise of a receding hairline, lanky arms,
a red-pine beard.
You're here to recover from a relationship.
Or to become the person you never were, as a character
in a German film, someone named Marion, dancing in European pubs,
searching for something she knows doesn't exist.

        In Somer, I have you say,
denk' ich am liebsten.
Or maybe you should speak *de diálogos espanoles,*

pequeños revueltas como la noche
llegue a ver tus expresiones
mientras haciamos el amor–

I suppose now I've created a displacement
with you and the verse, the same displacement I felt
during my college years, the same scenes I play back
as I try to drift into sleep, a self-induced sadism, a wanting
to change patterns of past events, the confusions,
the fumblings with sexuality. And see,

I've transformed these sentences,
so they no longer resemble a quilt,
or an embellished collage. They've become nothing
but a collection of ramblings,
broken metaphors,
myself trying too hard

to be Frank O'Hara
lost in another city.
Once, I've even tried to raise his shade,
to allow his light into my darkening rooms,
to apologize,
to idolize–

But now, let me step back,
find my place in this new moment,
of writing for you a poem of discovery,
of finding yourself wandering among emotions,
over confessionals in phone booths,
of flash and dagger nights,

with white wine and hoosier bars,
dancings with a poet who has given up on love
for the love of words, of images.
Years from now, do not forget the living
you have accomplished, the varieties of self gained–
Let these nights remain with you,

locked in eternal recollection,
the ghost of your youth linked
arm-in-arm with your present tense,
waltzing softly forward, with half steps,
inching ever closer to the ever present future,
his form lingering, waiting just on the edge of the horizon.

WINTER PERCUSSION:
DRUM SOLO

        1.

At first, it begins
      with the spot light missing its mark.
            Only a back-light exposes my head
with small moons of perspiration beading
      across the receding hairline, as if
            I were caught in a slight rainstorm,
my form unstill, fluid, and then
      the eccentric   epicenter
            opens out to the *rrrlll-bt-bt*,
rrrlll-bt-bt-rrrlll combination
      handshake / earthquake.
            The beat rains down
clashing against rusted gutters
      and tin-tiled roofs,
            volume increased,
the beat twisted beyond expectation,
      or last night's rehearsal
            in the basement of the old church
ts, ts, kah-ching slam, bam, ts-ts,
      but now thinking:
            I am possessed—
my past shifts tight within me quick,
      circling backwards. Transforming me
to Shiva with one hundred arms
      each hand holding a sacred tool—
            I become the god of
percussion. The world moves
      beneath me,   opening
and closing between tides:
      night to day, mathematic
            formulas. I become
a norse moon—pale,
      withdrawn, hovering over the
            landscape in winter months—

2.
Call this my one dark symphony
        a tribute to the persistence
                of unwanted memory, as
the arch of a raised fist,
        the force of a blow dropped
                against the snare—you know,

it's all the same, it all
        accumulates to *now*,
                to *balance* or *pivot*
follow the chain, unfold
        the events, one by one,
                back to the year ninety-eighty
when Mike and Steve beat on one of
        the newer kids—myself I mean,
                against me, the chosen victim,
chanting their slurs   *fag-got, fair-ry*
    smack-tish, slap-trill smack-tish, slap-trill–
                My rage bottled as a martyr
until the rage   let itself out
        when later I bloodied fingers,
                pounded knuckles against the school's
bathroom mirror—
        against the self
                reflecting back
but what more can be added to
        the story? Rage turns to *rifts* and
                staccato, pulse, words of a new
language. Words once unknown, hidden,
        emerge themselves.   Bobbing, weaving,
                a new image of self, something
other, you see. Something transformed.
        The rhythm internal   translated,
                the same way   God took up Elijah,

bodily, leaving no trace of him—
        What I mean   is that the changes stemmed
                from myself,   from what was already
existing in my hands, that unseen
        pulsing code,
                spiraling DNA
unfolding in the blood in my lungs
        despite the external chaotic
                challenges we all call living life—

3.

Handfuls of years later I bumped
into Michael   stumbling in the
dark, between bars,   blind drunk and lost
in a blind haze his life beaten
down to a bruise *you stand me man?*
he slurred -stan me? his hands groped for
a release of   circumstances
from the past, from   memories he
fought to forget his hands fumbling
with my jacket *listen to me*
a failed career, a failed marriage,
that same story— falling into
me, suddenly   erratic, drunk,
his life twisting his arm backwards,
his life laughing at his expressions
of pain, pounding him in the gut
not once, not twice,   but multiple
times, until the moment he stood
groping my clothes   leaning into
me for support not wanting to
fall back into   a present tense
of awareness— but I stepped back,
and he collapsed against a stool,
slumped over. Lost.   Odd, the lack of
feeling, even   now—

                    4.
falling to
          the present
                    tense. To *here*:
the stage lights,
          my motions
                    tripping cross
this warm room.
          Shadows leap
                    around, dance
as the lights
          point me out
                    a rhythmic
conundrum,
          chaos then
                    order, pulse
then silence—
          but not a silence
                    rather a static
whisper—metal brush
          across the cymbal
                    as ice trembling in the wind
or scraping across windows
          or fingertips on paper—
                    a softer rain than before,
falling unhesitantly,
          then, a slight rumbling
                    the final drum-roll
you know, the last avalanche
          of the night, the last   session
                    accumulation
of the past,
          land-slide, memories slipping down,
torrents of impressions,
          pages torn
                    from journals,
as a book divided,
          ripped in half,
                    unbound, an   explosion,
internal energy
          released, leaflets fall
                    scattered in the wind,
the blank manuscript
          that was my body
                    suddenly filled up,

overflowing with
        intense calligraphy
                musical notations,
and those
        imprecise histories—
                all that clutter that makes   us who we are, little

conflicting molecules,
        chaos theory released,
                galaxies colliding—
but then,
        the storm subsides,
                winds fade,
and mist gathers
        outside from the damp streets
                the murmuring audience
breathes again, falling back
        into their own patterns and memories,
                released.

PAUL PINKMAN

WOUNDED SOLDIER

PAUL PINKMAN graciously provided "Wounded Soldier," the cover art for this issue of *Assaracus*. Paul studied Art History and Art Studio at Seton Hall University. He followed this with graduate studies in Art History at Rutgers University. He has exhibited extensively throughout the Tri-state Area since the mid 1980s. His work has been included in a variety of shows in New York City including the Independents' Biennial, as well as in the New Jersey Arts Annual at the State Museum in Trenton and the Visual Arts Center of New Jersey in Summit. Articles about his work have been featured in *The New York Times*, *The Star Ledger*, *The Courier News* and in multiple places online. In addition, he has been a curator of exhibitions at the Watchung Arts Center (watchungarts.org) and a founding member of the New Art Group (newartgroup.com). Most recently his work has been exhibited at the University of North Carolina, Pembroke, the Monroe Center for Visual Arts in Hoboken and the Watchung Arts Center. Currently he resides in central New Jersey.

www.pinkmania.com

SUBMIT TO ASSARACUS

The mission of Sibling Rivalry Press is to develop, publish, and promote outlaw artistic talent—those projects which inspire people to read, challenge, and ponder the complexities of life in dark rooms, under blankets by cell-phone illumination, in the backseats of cars, and on spring-day park benches next to people reading Brass and Picano. We encourage submissions to *Assaracus* by gay male poets of any age, regardless of background, education, or level of publication experience. Submissions are accepted during the months of January, May, and September. For more information, visit us online.

SUBSCRIBE TO ASSARACUS

Readers can now subscribe to receive a year of *Assaracus*. The subscription price is $50.00 for U.S. readers and $80.00 for international readers (including shipping), which buys you four book-length (120+ pages), perfect-bound issues of our grand stage for gay contemporary poetry. Subscriptions are available through our website.

NEW FROM SIBLING RIVALRY PRESS

Sonics in Warholia by Megan Volpert: Speaking directly to the pop icon's ghost, Megan Volpert dives into a completely charted yet utterly unknown ocean that is Andy Warhol. The resulting collection of love letters and hate mail audaciously perforates the scene of the usual cultural suspects with icy shrapnel in a terrifying mirror game. This is not a biography, but a book that reflects Andy—detects him, the Andy who deflects. Working into territory that channels the essay as its more radical practitioners imagine, Megan revives the prose poem and rethinks herself. As the idea of a "real" Andy begins to decay, the author learns to invent him and discovers herself everywhere. Remaking this mythic man in the image of her own baggage, Megan gives us her most personal writing to date and a striking truth: everybody becomes Andy.

www.siblingrivalrypress.com

CPSIA information can be obtained at www.ICGtesting.com
Printed in the USA
LVOW11s1949231013
358280LV00003B/324/P